Copyright © 2021 by Janet C Harper

All rights reserved. No part of this book may be reproduced or used in any manner without written permission of the copyright owner. For more information, contact janet@thespanishcoach.net

FIRST PUBLISHED IN 2021
This edition: 1

ISBN: 978-1-80049-620-0

¡Hola! I'm Janet Harper, The Spanish Coach.

15 years ago, as I was starting out on my own journey learning Spanish, a friend asked if I'd teach her what I'd already learned in exchange for her cooking dinner. If anyone had told me at the time that one request would lead to me becoming a full time Spanish tutor, having taught several hundred students, I just wouldn't have believed them.

It's been an evolving journey. Most of my students are over the age of 35 (some of them a lot more!) and have been outside of a learning environment for several decades. They are not chasing a qualification, or working to a fixed timescale, but learning for pleasure because they live in or like to travel to Spain.

My emphasis has always been on *making learning fun* and a huge part of that has been thinking up amusing or quirky ways for my students to remember things… and they really seem to work!

Over the years they've become known to my students as **Janet's Rules** and I always said that one day I'd empty them out of my head and into a book, so here we are! This is not a "read-from-cover-to-cover-curriculum" for learning Spanish. This book is filled with my little tricks for pronunciation, memory joggers, top tips, rules and some frequently asked questions answered. This is not a conventional reference book, it is bite-sized learning that will help you join the pieces of the Spanish language jigsaw puzzle and become a handy study companion for your learning journey.

As the Spanish say: **¡espero que lo disfrute!** (I hope you enjoy it!)

To help you along your way:

Answers to my most frequently asked questions over the years

Explanations of some common Spanish language rules

Tips and tricks to help you remember things along the way

Little stories to give context to your Spanish learning

Contents

¡hola! Exchanging greetings	6
The "correct" hello Greeting people	6
Easing the learning journey with verbs	7
Who's who? A way to easily remember pronouns	7
Taking those first steps with the language	8
What do you look like? Physical descriptions	8
Meet the family	9
The Spanish alphabet	10
Pronunciation tips	11
What is your name?	12
Mastering the other 5% More pronunciation tips	12
Having a Spanish-themed evening Practicing at home	13
Masculine vs. Feminine	14
Mañana Syndrome Exploring the term	15
"How long will it take me to learn Spanish?"	15
Verbs, verbs, verbs Introducing ER, AR and IR verbs	16
What time is it?	17
A funny little verb called llevar Exploring its use	17
Make learning vocab as easy as ABC Building a vocab book	18
Tu and Tú Exploring the difference	18
That eternal question Understanding "por que" and "para que"	19
Me, myself & yo Understanding when to use "yo"	20
Manuel's favourite word Understanding the word "que"	20
My top five mistakes to avoid	21
The back-to-back rule Lining up verbs	21
Taking a look at muy vs. mucho	22
Why you should be a "Keepy Goer"	23
Meet DEL and AL Exploring contractions	23
The cautionary tale of the tuna sandwich Small victories	24
Linking your sentences together	25
Capital letters	25

Contents

This, that, these and those	26
The tale of a little dog Introducing diminutives	26
Lost for words? Don't panic! Buying time	27
Grab yourself a whiteboard	27
Everyone learns differently Start where best suits you	28
To know (part one) Exploring the verb CONOCER	29
How much & how many?	29
Top Tips for speaking Spanish like a native	30
To be or not to be Exploring the verb SER and the "Doctor list"	32
"Do" & "Don't" don't exist!	33
How a little French knife can help your grammar Looking at word order	33
To be or not to be Exploring the verb ESTAR and the "Place list"	34
Giving and asking for directions	35
Talking about possessions	35
Dealing with double negatives	36
Looking at our daily routine Exploring reflexive verbs	36
SER and ESTAR anomalies	39
Obligations Looking at "I have to..."	39
To know (part two) Exploring the verb SABER	40
SER & ESTAR More tips	40
I'm hungry Why we should use TENER	41
Two fewer words to learn	41
Is your motivation in hibernation? Tips for staying motivated	42
Looking into the future Introducing the future tense	43
What I want Looking at the verb QUERER	44
Oops I've made a mistake... Tips for when you make an error	44
Some notable exceptions Exceptions to the masculine/feminine rules	45
One final exception Finalising those masculine feminine rules	45
It's a back to front world More explorations of word order	46
Vocab clusters Tips for gathering lots of new words	46
How your home town can help with your conversations	47

Contents

Learn your Spanish verbs in a flash Looking at using flashcards — 48
Age is just a number Talking about ages — 48
Let he who is without sin The difference between "no" and "sin" — 49
The two ways of spending Looking at GASTAR and PASAR — 49
Exactly who are you talking about? Exploring "Quién" — 50
Typing tildes Tips for writing accents when typing — 50
Pleased to meet you How to greet in Spanish — 51
The verb game A game to help practice your verbs — 51
Talking about our likes and dislikes — 52
Why you should be a little more Amy... Tips for improving your Spanish — 53
A look at POR and PARA — 54
Why you shouldn't be afraid to strike up a conversation — 55
Tips to improve your listening skills (part one) — 56
A stem, a stem-change and a boot? Tips for irregular verbs — 57
Tips to improve your listening skills (part two) — 58
Notes — 59

¡hola!

Exchanging greetings and finding out a few basic bits of information is a great way to start to "dip a toe" into the language!

But first, an insight into how those greetings might look in the written form...

¡hola!

It's a word that almost everyone on the planet might recognise (just in case you don't, it's 'hello') but what about those funny looking exclamation marks before and after?

The "!" at the end we recognise. It tells us the word is to be said *with feeling*. As you've no doubt noticed, the Spanish are very passionate in the way that they speak (hands waving, voices raised) and it's the same with their written words too...

So to help us out, they not only put the exclamation mark after the word (or words), they put an upside-down one in front of the word too, as a kind of warning of what's to come.

In the same way, when asking a question an upside-down question mark goes upfront and a normal one sits at the end of the question. This is particularly handy when reading Spanish, you know at the start of a sentence that you are reading a question...

¿cómo estás?

(how are you?)

In Spanish, you're never in any doubt that this is a question or an exclamation!

The "correct" hello...

Sticking with the subject of greeting people... You might not even think about it, but the way we greet people in English can depend on how well we know them. We do it so automatically that we probably don't even realise it's happening (and if it's any consolation, it will very quickly become like that in Spanish too!)

Let's look at an example. If you bump into a good friend, you'd no doubt say something like **"hiya, how's you?"** whereas if you were going into an interview you'd want to be a bit more formal. Without thinking, your greeting would become **"good morning, how are you?"**

The same is true with Spanish-speaking people...

Meeting a good friend
Hiya, how's you?
¡Hola! ¿qué tal?

Walking into an interview
Good morning, how are you?
buenos dias ¿cómo está usted?

Meeting an everyday acquaintance
Hello, how are you?
¡Hola! ¿cómo estás?

 *Notice that by adding an "s" to the **estás** it makes it less formal (...and yes, they do notice - even at the high speed that they speak!)

This is such a good place to start when using the language! Try each of them out as soon as you can.

Which feels more comfortable to use? Maybe you're a relaxed "everyone is my friend" kind of person, in which case a **¿qué tal?** is perfect for you. It's all about developing your style.

Listen out for greetings too. Try "mirroring" what you are greeted with, but definitely don't get hung up on getting it wrong. There is no right or wrong on this topic!

Easing the learning journey with verbs...

As part of my teaching method, as far as possible, I try to avoid using grammatical terms in class. My students prefer it that way. Almost without exception they've said that all the talk of nouns, adjectives, pronouns and conjugating verbs has put them off learning in a typical classroom or online program.

That seems such a tragedy to me. Missing out on the sounds and passion of the language because someone wanted you to learn it the "proper" way.

It's at that point I entered centre stage to change some of those outdated ideas and make the language accessible for all. Strangely, "verbs" is one grammatical term which didn't get put on the scrap heap. We talk through in class that they are things we do and that works just fine.

You'll see one of my "adaptations" over on the right of this page with my "who's who" list. Another trick I use is called my **"verb list"**...

(line one)	**yo** hablo
(line two)	**tú** hablas
(line three)	**él/ella** habla
(line four)	**nosotros** hablamos
(line five)	**vosotros** habláis
(line six)	**ellos/ellas** hablan

Now, we could call the "yo" line "first person singular" and the "ellos/ellas" line "third person plural" or we could simply number the lines of the verb 1-6!

So as you work through this book, you will see I often refer to various "lines" of a verb... and now you know why. As I always say...

KISS
Keep It Simple Spanish!

Who's who?

In this case, who's who when we are talking about **verbs**...

As my students would tell you, as far as possible I tend to avoid "grammatical" terms in class. Not to be over-simplistic, it's just the relaxed way my students seem to prefer.

As an example, when we start to focus on the use of **verbs** (yes, we can't really escape that one!), instead of talking **pronouns**, we use the "who's who list." This is the list of "who" might be "doing" a particular activity within a sentence. Let's take a look at the list...

- **Yo** - I
- **Tú** - you (singular)
- **Él/ella** - he/she
- **Nosotros** – we
- **Vosotros** - you (plural)
- **Ellos/ellas** - they

This is then followed by the **verb** which, as you may know, has its own ending depending on who we're talking about.

Let's take a look at an example using the verb **hablar** (meaning "to speak")...

- **Yo habl**o - I speak
- **Tú habl**as - you speak
- **Él/ella habl**a - he/she speaks
- **Nosotros habl**amos - we speak
- **Vosotros habl**áis - you speak
- **Ellos/ellas habl**an - they speak

Taking those first steps with the language...

My advice is always don't put off until tomorrow what you can do today. The sooner you start to *use* the language, the sooner you will become fluent at it. Don't think "I will start when I'm better/good enough" because that day will keep slipping further and further into the future ...and your confidence along with it.

So today (yes, literally today), start from where you are at. Whether its a handful of words, or even a sentence, it's a start and you have something to build on tomorrow.

Make some flashcards with some basic 'get by' sentences. English on one side and Spanish on the other. Keep them handy and practice them often. Here are a few to get you going:

Estoy aprendiendo español
I am learning Spanish (this will help you out of SO many situations, the Spanish love to encourage people who are learning).

No comprendo
I don't understand

¿me comprendes?
Do you understand me?

puedes hablar lentamente
Can you speak slowly

¿Como se dice...?
How does one say...

¿Qué significa eso ...?
What does ... mean?

Puedes ayudarme
Can you help me

Right then...are you ready?

What do you look like?

Here are some useful words for physical descriptions to add to your vocabulary stash. (Keep an eye on how the describing words have the masculine/feminine option!)

- Tall **alto/a**
- Short **bajo/a**
- Medium height **estatura media**
- Thin **delgado/a**
- Fat **gordo/a**
- Blonde **rubio/a**
- Dark hair **moreno/a**
- Long hair **pelo largo**
- Short hair **pelo corto**
- Eyes: blue/brown/green **ojos azules/marrónes/verdes**

So now that we have the ingredients, let's create some descriptions...

Soy alta y delgada
I am tall and thin (remember, we use the our friend **ser** when we are "describing")

Tengo pelo corto y rubio
I have short blonde hair

Mis ojos son verdes
my eyes are green

CHALLENGE:

You are meeting someone at the airport. You've not met them before and they have asked for your description, so they know who to look out for.

How would you describe yourself for them?

Meet the family
(and remember them easily!)

In my last book, **Practice Makes Perfect: Coffee break puzzles***, I shared loads of new vocabulary to help expand and improve your Spanish. One of those topics was naming different family members.

In that book we saw how the Spanish words for male and female members of the family are almost always the same word with just one letter being different. Usually, the words for male family members end in "O" and females members end in "A". Therefore we only need to learn half as much vocabulary – now there's a bit of good news!

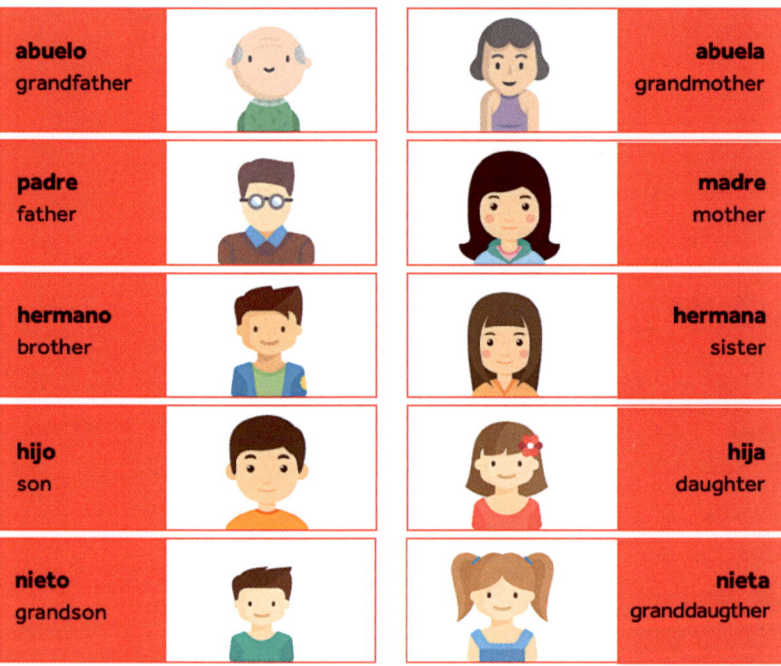

If we wanted to take that one step further and talk collectively about family members, for example grandparents, parents, siblings etc, we simply take the 'male' word and make it plural…

- o Grandparents are **abuelos**
- o Parents are **padres**
- o Brothers and sisters are **hermanos**

*Have you got your copy yet? It's an excellent way to expand your Spanish vocabulary! Order yours now at www.thespanishcoach.net/store

The Spanish alphabet:
It's not just for spelling...

Yes, that sounds like a strange thing to say, but because the Spanish language is phonetic we say what we see. That might sound like we're on an episode of Catchphrase, but that's literally how it works!

In English things are more complicated. For example, the letter **E** can make many different sounds depending on where it sits within the word. Take "bed", that's the E making an "eh" sound, but when it's placed next to another E, for example in "need", that's now an "eeeee" sound. Sometimes (like BOTH times it appears in the word "sometimes") it is completely silent!

The Spanish alphabet is so much more straightforward. Generally speaking (there are a *few* exceptions we'll come to later), each letter has its own sound and once you've mastered those, you simply sound them all out in turn and you can correctly pronounce any word. Let's take a look at the full alphabet and the "sounds" of each character. Notice how the Spanish alphabet has 29 characters, three more than the English one, each with their own unique sounds.

A aah	**B** bay	**C** thay	**CH** chay	**D** day	**E** eh
F efay	**G** hay	**H** achay	**I** ee	**J** hotta	**K** kah
L ellay	**LL** ey-yay	**M** emay	**N** enay	**Ñ** en-yay	**O** oh
P pay	**Q** coo	**R** erray	**S** essay	**T** tey	**U** ooo
V ubay	**W** ubay-doblay	**X** eh-kiss	**Y** ig-ree-egg-ah	**Z** theta	

The number of times you'll need to recite the alphabet are probably zero, but it is useful to learn how to spell your name or your street name - plus in Spain your identity number has letters at the beginning and the end, so that's going to pick up a few letters from the alphabet. Learning the whole thing gets it over with now, rather than catching you out later!

Pronunciation Tips
(...and avoiding ¿qué? face!)

Picture the scene. You're determined to start putting your new language into use and the perfect opportunity presents itself - you have to ask for something at the post office or the bank.

You've planned ahead by checking any vocab you're uncertain about, maybe even written it on a piece of paper that you're clutching on to. You get to the front of the queue and blurt out your well-rehearsed spiel. Go you. You're such a winner. There are a few moments of silence and then the girl behind the counter looks at you as if a red mist has suddenly descended, screws up her face and says ¿qué...?

We've all been there at some point, believe me! There is actually a cool little "rule" which can eliminate that happening for around 95% of your Spanish (that's a pretty good success rate in my book!) So here goes...

First, we'll go back to our school days (which is further back than we'd care to remember for some of us...) and refresh our memory of the vowels. That's **a e i o u**. In Spanish, these are such a big part of pronunciation.

Now, stay with me whilst I take this a step further. Let's take the Spanish word **estupendo** (it means "great" or "wonderful"). Break it down into syllables: *es – too – pen - doh*. Great, we are on the way to getting it right.

But here's the clever bit...

- Go to the end of the word and, counting backwards, we pick on the last-but-one vowel (in this case, it's the E)
- We are going to *stretch* that E sound, to really emphasise that syllable.
- This gives us *es-too-PEN-doh*... really stretching out and emphasising that PEN (as in PENNY).

That's it! We simply pick the last-but-one vowel, lift our voice a little and *stretch* it out!

Now it's your turn...

Practice it - pick a Spanish word, search out the last-but-one vowel and *stretch* it out!

- **ca**sa (house) is **caaa**-sa
- **li**bro (book) is **Liii**-bro
- estu**dia**nte (student) is est-you-di-**aaan**-tay

What is your name?

Another subject for those vital "getting to know you" conversations would definitely be finding out someone's name.

As in English, there are two commonly used routes for this, let's look at each individually.

¿cuál es tu nombre?

Which means "what is your name?" The actual translation is "which" is your name? The thinking being, of all the names that are out there, which one is yours?!

To this version, you would reply **mi nombre es...** (my name is...)

¿cómo te llamas?

This time we are asking "what are you called?" and to this you would reply **me llamo...** (I call myself...)

Look at that double L! Whenever we see LL we pronounce it as a Y - so this sentence phonetically is "como tay yamas"

We'll be looking a bit deeper at pronunciation a little later in the book...

Mastering that other 5%...

Following on from my earlier little rule about pronunciation... do you remember me saying that it'd cure 95% of your spoken words?

Well, I'm a 100% kind of a girl, so how can we improve on that previous pass rate? With another little Spanish Coach Rule, that's how!

You've probably noticed that quite a few words in Spanish have an accent (or "tilde") over some letters? For example...

- **adiós** ("goodbye")
- **estás** ("you are" or "are you")
- **lápiz.** ("pencil")

If a word has a tilde, we can forget the last-but-one vowel rule and instead we now *stretch* the vowel with the tilde above it. That's actually why it's there, to remind us "emphasise here". (In fact, that's why in English we call them "accents", because we *accentuate* that part of the word.)

So those words we looked at are pronounced...

- **adiós:** ad-i-OOOs
- **estás:** eh-stAAAs
- **lápiz:.** lAAA-piz

That's it! You've got the secret recipe to good pronunciation. After all, after taking the trouble to learn and remember these words, it makes sense to master the final part of the formula to help us on the way to effective communication, right?

Why having a Spanish-themed evening can really help your learning...

Story time

A brilliant way to practice your Spanish is to have a "Spanish Evening" at home with the family or some friends. Perhaps you are learning as a couple or your children are in a Spanish speaking school? If you have a Study Buddy maybe you could do this together for one of your practice sessions? As I always say, "practice makes perfect!"

Get right into the Spanish atmosphere with a good bottle of Spanish rioja, maybe stream some Gypsy Kings in the background, and make some traditional tapas to share. Trust me, the atmosphere genuinely makes a difference!

This is one of my favourite tapas dishes – **patatas bravas**, or "spicy potatoes". They are so easy to prepare and will give your evening a really authentic feel...

INGREDIENTS:

The sauce

3 tbsp olive oil
1 small onion
2 cloves of garlic, chopped
227g can chopped tomatoes
1 tbsp tomato purée
2 tsp smoked paprika
Good pinch of chilli powder
Pinch sugar
Chopped fresh parsley to garnish

The potatoes

900g potatoes, cut into small cubes
2 tbsp olive oil

METHOD:

Heat the oil in a pan and fry the onion for about 5 mins until softened. Add the garlic, chopped tomatoes, tomato purée, sweet paprika, chilli powder, sugar and salt, then bring them to the boil, stirring occasionally.

Lower to a simmer and cook for 10mins until rich and pulpy. This sauce can be kept chilled for up to 24hrs. Great if you want to get prepared in advance!

Heat your oven to 180C. Pat the potatoes dry with kitchen paper, then tip into a roasting tin and toss in the olive oil and some seasoning. Roast for 40 – 50 mins until crisp and golden.

Tip the potatoes into serving dishes and spoon over the sauce. Sprinkle with some fresh parsley and/or sour cream to serve. Simply **delicioso**!

Masculine vs. Feminine: What's that all about?

That's a really good question and one that comes up often. Having words that are deemed "masculine" and "feminine" is not a concept within our native English language (although it's common in the majority of other languages), so it's a new concept to get our heads around when learning Spanish.

Putting the *why* to one side for a moment, it is something that is a huge part of the Spanish language and so important to get right. Enter stage-left my next little "rule" to help sort the girls from the boys via a collection of "pots"... (I know, here she goes again!) To illustrate I'm going to use 3 different fruits...

manzana

plátano

limón

Firstly, I'm going to line up three pots. Two are regular size and the third is much bigger. Into the the first pot I'm going to put my **manzana** along with all the Spanish words I know **which end in A**. (**la casa, la chica, la mesa, la falda, la ventana**). **Most words that end in A are feminine.** You will have spotted that the word "the" for feminine things is **la**. Therefore "the apple" is **la manzana**.

Into my second pot I'll put my **plátano** along with all the Spanish words I know **which end in O** (**el libro, el vino, el chico, el zapato**). **Most words which end in O are masculine**. You will have spotted that the word "the" for masculine things is **el**. Therefore "the banana" is **el plátano**.

The third pot was our biggie, because into that goes all the other words we know that **end in letters other than A and O** (coche, bar, árbol, móvil). Words in this pot are going to be treated as masculine (for now) the same as pot two, which means our "the" will again be **el**. Therefore, "the lemon" is **el limón**.

Now I can guess what you're thinking, why not just have two pots? One for A's and one for the rest. I know, but there is a good reason for not doing so... plurals. When things in pot one are talked about in the plural, **la manzana** becomes **las manzanas,** an S is added to both words. Over in pot two, **el plátano** becomes **los plátanos** - this time the "el" has changed completely and becomes a plural "los" and an S has been added to plátano.

Now here's the reason why the third pot is needed. **El limón** becomes **los limónes.** Not only has the "el" changed to "los", but this time we've added an ES to the lemon.

And this is the secret. **Everything in that third pot (things that don't end in A or O), need an "es" added when they go plural!** Now, this rule *does* have exceptions but there are so few it's really not worth worrying about them at this stage. We will come to those later...

"Mañana" Syndrome

Mañana is a very well-known Spanish word. Some say it truly sums up the laid back Spanish culture (nothing is too important that it can't wait until "tomorrow!"). Others jokingly say "the word doesn't mean tomorrow, it simply means not today!"

Jokes aside, I am often asked the meaning of the phrase "**mañana por la mañana**". Before I answer that one, we need to rewind a little. Firstly, let's have a look at the Spanish word for "the day" - that's **el dia**.

You may be looking at that thinking "it ends in an A so why isn't it the feminine "la dia?" Well, that's the first mystery. *A whole day is masculine* therefore **el dia**. *Parts of the day are feminine* for example **mañana** (morning), **tarde** (afternoon) and **noche** (evening/night) regardless of what their endings are. So it's **la mañana**, **la tarde** and **la noche**.

Did you notice **mañana** by itself means "tomorrow", but preceded by **por la** means "in the morning."

- To say "in the morning" we use **por la mañana**
- To say "in the afternoon" we use **por la tarde**
- To say "in the evening" we use **por la noche**

To return to our original question...

- **mañana por la mañana** means tomorrow in the morning
- **mañana por la noche** means tomorrow in the evening

Taking that one more step further...

- **Sábado por la tarde** means Saturday afternoon
- **Domingo por la mañana** means Sunday morning

Before you say it, yes I agree - there is a strange mix of rules here, but if you stick to the rules (and try to forget the logic!) it becomes a lot easier!

"How long will it take me to learn Spanish?"

Well, that is definitely one of my most frequently asked questions by new students. Broadly, my answer invariably begins with "it will depend on what level of Spanish you are hoping to achieve."

If you're only expecting to ask for the small stuff, or begin a friendly little chat, you can realistically learn the common expressions (and the replies that come with them) quite quickly. Most students have these memorised in only a few months.

However, if you're looking to acquire some true **conversation** you have to realistically give yourself up to a year, depending on how dedicated you are and how quickly you can grasp the concepts.

Actually **using the language** with people who speak it is a challenge in itself and that can take a long time.

Learning the basics of **grammar** is essential to develop your conversational skills, in preparation for the second phase.

Attending **conversation groups** speeds up the process immensely. You can practice your new language, get corrected, expand your vocabulary... all at the same time!

I always say...

"**Treat the learning process as a journey to be travelled. Enjoy and celebrate the successes along the way. Practice often and try not to watch the clock or the calendar in terms of *am I there yet?*"**

Verbs...verbs...verbs!

You will have seen so far that, as much as possible, I avoid "grammatical chatter" in favour of simpler, more "day-to-day" terminology to KISS (keep it simple Spanish!) That being said, **verbs** kind of sit in a class of their own, an exception to that rule. Beyond knowing that they are "doing" words, typically ending in -ing in English (walking, talking, eating, singing etc), they are the backbone of every language and we need them to build sentences.

So, let's look at some **regular verbs**. These are verbs that all follow a regular pattern and, once learnt, we can simply apply that regular pattern to any regular verb. (As you might have guessed, that does imply the existence of "irregular verbs" – those that don't follow a set pattern. We'll come back to those later.)

Regular verbs can be split into three groups, they will all end in either **AR**, **ER** or **IR**. We'll start with an example from the first group, **hablar** – an "AR" verb meaning *to speak*.

- Firstly we take off the AR ending, leaving **habl**. This is called the "stem".
- Onto the stem we add an ending which is unique to whomever is speaking (see below).
- Now the good news: these same three sets of endings are the same for all regular verbs. Once you've mastered them, you can use them with any regular verb.

"AR" VERBS HABLAR: to speak	"ER" VERBS COMER: to eat	"IR" VERBS VIVIR: to live
yo hablo I speak	**yo como** I eat	**yo vivo** I live
tú hablas you speak	**tú comes** you eat	**tú vives** you live
él/ella habla he/she speaks	**él/ella come** he/she eats	**él/ella vive** he/she lives
nosotros hablamos we speak	**nosotros comemos** we eat	**nosotros vivimos** we live
vosotros habláis you (pl) speak	**vosotros coméis** you (pl) eat	**vosotros vivís** you (pl) live
ellos/ellas hablan they speak	**ellos/ellas comen** they eat	**ellos/ellas viven** they live

You may have spotted that the **IR** verbs have *almost* the same set of endings as the **ER** verbs, but the **nosotros** and **vosotros** lines replace the E with an I. Getting to grips with this formula forms a HUGE part of the language and taking the time to master it early on will really pay dividends later on.

What time is it?

It is so useful to master this subject. For making appointments, meeting people or simply if you're asked the question, time is such a big part of our lives, so let's sort it out!

Firstly, to ask "what time is it? " we say **¿qué hora es?** Taken quite literally, we are asking "what hour is it?"

If we wanted to reply that it's 2 o'clock, we'd say **son las dos** (the **las** in front of the number tells the listener we're talking "time" and not just saying "it is two").

- 2.15pm therefore becomes **son las dos y cuarto**
- 2.20pm is **son las dos y veinte**
- 2.30pm is **son las dos y media**

All the increments between o'clock and half past will be the hour "y" (and) however many minutes.

As the minute hand begins its trip back to the top of the clock, we take the number of the next hour less (**menos**) however many minutes...

- 3:45pm is **son las cuatro menos cuarto**
- 3:50pm is **son las cuatro menos diez**

So there you go, once you've got your numbers mastered, you'll be telling the time like a local!

Here's a little Spanish Coach tip for learning to tell the time really quickly...

Each time your check your watch, clock or phone to see the time, say it in Spanish, even if only by talking to yourself in your head. You'll soon have it mastered!

A funny little verb called llevar...

It's a funny little verb because it is used in so many strange ways. First let us look at the pronunciation. **Llevar** = yay-bar.

It means "to carry" or "to wear." They don't really seem to be connected, do they? Let me explain with some examples...

Takeaway food is **comida para llevar,** food that you literally "carry away". That works... and we "carry" our clothes around with us as we "wear" them. Let's continue...

hoy estoy llevando una camiseta roja
today I am wearing a red t-shirt

See how I've turned the *wear* into *wearing* by adding the "ando" ending onto the stem.

A great 2-for-1 activity to practice this new verb and some vocab at the same time is to list what you are wearing today. Firstly let's pull up some **vocabulario de ropas** (clothes vocabulary) so that we have something to practice with...

- **Los pantalones** trousers
- **El vestido** dress
- **La falda** skirt
- **Los vaqueros** jeans
- **La camiseta** t-shirt
- **Los zapatos** shoes
- **Los pantalones cortes** shorts

Now you can create your list. Starting with **hoy estoy llevando...**

Why not add the colour of each item too (remembering to get the masculine/feminine of the colour matching the item of clothing).

Each morning, as you get dressed, talk this through in your head, **hoy estoy llevando...**

The more you think like a Spanish person the more the magic starts to happen! Practice whenever and wherever you can, even if it's just in your head!

Make learning vocab as easy as A...B...C...

On our learning journey we are going to encounter a mountain of new vocabulary. During our early lessons we write them in our notebooks and as we progress we start another notebook and so on.

All those "new words" are at risk of getting lost in a sea of scribbled note-taking. We've all been in the situation of thumbing backwards and forwards through notes... "I know I've written it in here... *somewhere!*"

My top tip is to start early with a simple but hugely effective little purchase: an A-Z index notebook. I'm not just saying this because I have a love of stationery (although I do!) but this little pocket diamond will become the one place you know exactly where to find all those new words. No more hunting!

Any good stationery supplier, or Amazon, will have a range of notebooks with A-Z indexed pages, from small pocket sized up to A4. Take your pick and start your own personal dictionary.

Draw a line down the centre of the page and list your new words in English on the left, with their Spanish translations on the right. **Apple = manzana, After = después**... and so on through the alphabet.

Each time you learn a new word (in class, out and about, something you overheard in a conversation), record it, don't waste it! Pop it into your A-Z book and over time you will have created your own personal dictionary of words you have already used and will no doubt use again.

Finally, my little warning: writing words down doesn't (necessarily) mean you'll remember them. The magic happens when you regularly make time to go through revising and testing yourself until they become familiar friends !

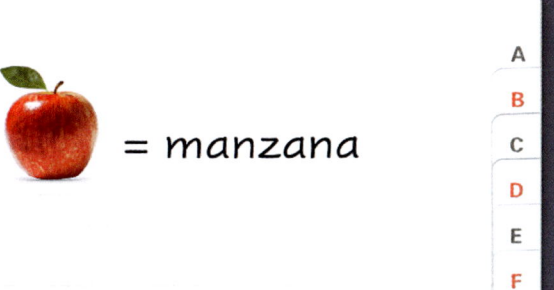

Tu and Tú = confusion?

Yes, it has been said! **Tu** means "your", whereas **tú** means "you".

When written, you can see one has the tilde, so that could make it easier to solve. However in the spoken form... HELP! Don't panic. Time to dust off another of "Janet's Rules"

Tú

is always followed by a verb. Coincidently, line two of a verb.

Tu

is always followed by a thing, i.e. something that is yours (coche, casa, perro etc)

It's quite black and white, one or the other.

This is a good time to introduce the idea of starting to listen to **blocks of a sentence** rather than trying to translate each word as it comes to you. Generally, as the sentence unfolds you will get the gist, if not all of the content.

That eternal question... ¿por qué? (or should that be ¿pará qué?)

¿pará qué? or **¿por qué?** Which is it? They both mean "why"...

This is a question that often comes up in my Training Room... and my response is generally "that's just the way it is!" Jokes aside, the use of **why** in Spanish needs a little bit of further explanation, as you will see. While both do indeed translate as "why", they both have different functions...

¿por qué?

Use ¿por qué? when you want to find out a reason.

¿por qué necesitas tanto dinero?
"why do you need so much money?"

Porque voy a comprar los palos de golf
"because I am buying golf clubs"

 Expect **porque** (because) in reply to your question.

¿pará qué?

Use ¿pará qué? to ask a purpose, literally "for what?"

¿pará qué necesitas tanto dinero?
"why do you need so much money?"

Para comprar los palos de golf
"(in order) to buy golf clubs"

 This time, expect **para** in reply to your question.

It's a very subtle difference isn't it?

In English the one word "why?" would suit both scenarios. When I was learning, I found writing out examples like these above help to cement the differences into my mind. As I always say "practice makes..." well, you know that saying by now!

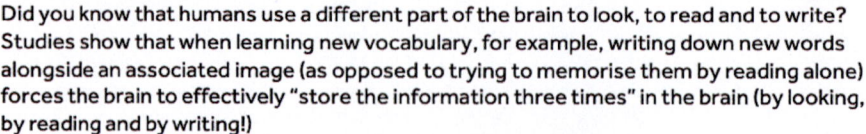

Improving your memory: the rule of three...

Did you know that humans use a different part of the brain to look, to read and to write? Studies show that when learning new vocabulary, for example, writing down new words alongside an associated image (as opposed to trying to memorise them by reading alone) forces the brain to effectively "store the information three times" in the brain (by looking, by reading and by writing!)

This significantly improves memory recall. How amazing is that!

Me, myself & yo

So here's a question I get asked a lot: "do I need to use **yo** when the statement already includes the YO form?"

For instance, why bother saying **yo estudio español** when **estudio español** already implies that we are talking about ourselves. Both statements mean "I study Spanish", so why say the "I" part twice?

Well first off, I say congratulations! The question shows the student has just identified an important aspect of the Spanish language. You don't need to use the "yo". It is in fact optional. Native Spanish speakers will tell you that you'll never sound natural in the language if you use "yo" unnecessarily.

So then why bother at all you may ask?

As I say, it is optional but it is not wrong either way. In, or out. As a general rule of thumb, I encourage students to use the "yo" when they are initially learning their verbs. It serves as a reminder to themselves that " yo" is the partner to "hablo" and I am talking about myself.

I believe it is easier to learn where pronouns go by using them, and then omitting them later should we choose!

Manuel's favourite word…

Remember that "little man from Barcelona?" His favourite word was **¿qué?** He used it all the time and no wonder - it has so many meanings! Here are just a few…

When referring to a person…
- La chica **que** habla con Juan es mi hermana
  The girl who is talking with Juan is my sister.

When referring to a thing…
- El libro **que** está en la mesa es mío
  The book which (that) is on the table is mine

 In English, we do not always use the words 'that' or 'which'. In Spanish, it is always stated.

Moving on, and adding an accent (or "tilde") the word **¿qué?** turns it into the questioning "what" or "how"…

- **¿qué tal?** How are you?
- **¿qué hora es?** What time is it?
- **¿qué?** Simply, what??

That little "tilde" changes the whole picture, so it's really important to get into the habit of using these right from the word go!

As you can see, there are lots of variations to this little word **que**, as Manuel himself would agree!

My top five mistakes to avoid...

Top Tip!

Whether you're a beginner or not, when the initial excitement of learning Spanish subsides we all find ourselves picking up some limiting habits. Do any of these sound familiar?

"I'll wait until I'm good enough..."

I always encourage students to use what they have learnt right from day one. If you wait until you are "good enough" you might never get started! Unlike in the UK where we are traditionally reserved, the Spanish love to exchange a smile and a greeting... in a lift, a queue in the bank, the cashier at the supermarket. Try this with "strangers" you see often. As your confidence grows (and it will the more you do this) find out their name and use it, maybe ask where they are from.

"I don't like it when I'm corrected..."

Never be put off by this. Making mistakes is how we grow, so embrace the help! Don't be afraid.

"My hour a week class is enough for me..."

Yes, you will learn the language, but it will be a *slow* journey. As with most things in life, you get out what you put in and 10-15 minutes every day will put you in the fast lane! So decide a time of day that works best for you... maybe it's with that first cup of coffee in the morning. Make it a date. Six or seven days of the week and you won't believe the difference it makes!

"I've no time... before I know it, it's bedtime!"

Yes, we all have full lives, even students who are retired tell me their days are always full. As in the previous point, I believe success comes by scheduling a time of day that works for you and (as much as possible) *set it in stone!* Once it's done you'll feel so accomplished rather than deflated at the "I haven't practised" end of the day.

"All the Spanish people I meet want to practise their English!"

Yes, I hear this one a lot, but the solution is very simple. Living in a tourist resort (as I do), the locals need to speak English. I always reply "you can speak English and I will practise my Spanish. Let's help each other!" It always works! Secondly, venture out! Find somewhere for tapas and practise with the waiters. Always be conscious of how busy they are though, if they're rushed off their feet wait until next time!

The back-to-back rule

My **back-to-back rule** is one of those rare "always rules" to remember.

Often in conversation we will need to line up two verbs together and this little rule (albeit short and simple) will remind you how to stack them when forming your sentence.

Let's look at an example...

"I want to learn Spanish"

There are two verbs in this sentence, "to want" & "to learn". The two verbs are back-to-back, there is nothing separating them. Let's call "to want" verb one and "to learn" verb two.

VERB ONE

When constructing our sentence we make verb one fit who is "doing the wanting". In this case it is "I want" - so **quiero**.

VERB TWO

Once we have established who verb one is referring to, we **always** show verb two in its full form. In this case it is "to learn" – **aprender.**

So now we have our completed sentence...

Yo quiero aprender español

Another example...

	(1)	(2)	
"I	like	to speak	Spanish"
me	gusta	hablar	español

Taking a look at MUY vs. MUCHO...

Delving back into my bag of "frequently asked questions" for a moment, another popular one is **"what is the difference between muy and mucho?"**

To answer that question, let's have a look at them both individually and the rules on how and when to use them. I've even got a little challenge at the end to test your learning. Let's start with muy, the more straightforward of the pair!

MUY

We use **muy** - meaning *very* - when we are talking **quantity**, to increase the intensity of something. It's easy to use because it's not affected by masculine or feminine or singles/plurals, and it sits in front of a describing word. Let's take a look at some examples...

- **Él es muy alto**   he is very tall
- **El café está muy caliente**   the coffee is very hot
- **El restaurante está muy lejos de aqui**   the restaurant is (very) far from here

MUCHO

This one means "a lot." When it is used after a verb, only the form mucho is used...

- **Ellos trabajan mucho**   they work a lot
- **Ella viaja mucho**   she travels a lot
- **¿lees mucho?**   do you read a lot?

...but when **mucho** is used in a describing way, we must remember to pick up and match the masculine/feminine/singular/plural of the thing(s) we are describing.

- **Tengo muchos libros**   I have a lot of books
- **Él quiere mucha comida**   he wants a lot of food
- **Aqui hay muchas personas**   there are many people here
- **Muchas gracias**   many thanks

Now it's your turn – give these a go!

1. No me siento .... bien   I don't feel well
2. Tengo .... frio   I am very cold
3. Ella habla ....   She talks a lot
4. Hay .... comida en la nevera   There is a lot of food in the fridge
5. Ellos cantan .... bien   They sing very well
6. Lo siento ....   I am really sorry
7. Rusia es un pais .... grande   Russia is a very big place
8. En el zoo hay .... animales   There are many animals in the zoo

Answers: 1. Muy 2. Mucho 3. Mucho 4. Mucha 5. Muy 6. Mucho 7. Muy 8. Muchos
How did you do?

Why you should be a "Keepy Goer..."

Anyone can start something, but it's the **keepy goers** that succeed!

Remember when you first decided you wanted to learn Spanish? Maybe it was just after moving to your new home in Spain and you felt it was an important factor in integrating into the Spanish community? Maybe you'd been an expat for a while, taking some time to settle into your new life before the time was right? Maybe you have a Spanish holiday home and fancied the challenge of learning the language so that you could converse with confidence in restaurants and enhance your holiday experience?

Whatever the reason for starting, no doubt in those early weeks and months the excitement of getting started and making steady progress kept you motivated and focused. It's definitely easier with that "new starter" wind in your sails. In the weeks and months since however, maybe the learning curve turned into a continual uphill challenge and the sparkle started to dull?

That's when we need to put on our "keepy goer" hat and dig in for the long haul. There is no quick fix or shortcut to becoming fluent. I never sugar coat the story... but the rewards that come along as you become more proficient are so amazing. Many of my students tell me stories that support this fact. Like this one...

> I went to a local Spanish restaurant and the waiter didn't speak any English. I managed to order and speak a little. The waiter understood and we had a little conversation. What a buzz! Eight lessons in and I'm actually speaking Spanish and being understood!

One of the many things I love about my work is when I hear how students take their first shaky steps in Spanish, get a small win and then go from strength to strength. It really feels better than winning the lottery when you have that first "proper conversation!"

So think back often to that reason which first motivated you to learn. It was your motivation for a reason. Keep that "why" in the front of your mind when you're feeling like throwing in the towel because, as I said at the start, it's the keepy goers that succeed!

Meet DEL and AL...

Have you ever seen either of these words used and wondered what they meant?

del   al

Well, first things first. Without getting too technical, these are called "contractions" (fortunately they are less painful than the kind that signals the arrival of a baby!)

We have them in English too. For example we have the words **do** and **not** but usually roll them together and simply say **don't**. It is exactly the same in Spanish. Let's look at some examples...

de (of/from)
+
el (the)
=
del

tengo una carta del banco
(I have a letter from the bank)

a (to/at)
+
el (the)
=
al

voy a ir al supermercado
(I am going to the supermarket)

The cautionary tale of the toasted tuna salad sandwich...

Story time

I stopped at one of my regular Spanish coffee bars recently...

After giving my order, I had a quick conversation with the owner. When we'd finished the conversation, a lady on the next table smiled across at me and said (in English) "your Spanish is excellent, can you tell me how I order my tuna salad toastie without tomato, in Spanish."

Many foreigners never make the effort to order anything complicated in Spanish, so I was pleased to help and spent a couple of minutes helping her say **"¿me das un sándwich con ensalada de atún sin tomate, por favor?"** She repeated it after me, and after a few attempts I smiled and said "great, you've got it!"

When the waiter came to her she hesitated, looked nervous and (looking a bit sheepish) switched to English: "can I have a toasted tuna salad sandwich but can you leave out the tomato, thanks". The waiter clearly didn't understand what she had asked for as, sure enough, when the sandwich arrived, I could see it contained tomato.

I watched her take out the tomato slices but didn't say anything.

The problem is that most people give up on Spanish without sticking at it for long enough.

Learning a language is about small victories - where every single day you use more and more Spanish sentences and gradually make yourself understood. Sentences that seem long and hard at first, quickly become easy once you've used them a few times.

Think about a scenario you might find yourself in, and how you might make your request in Spanish. Think it through, write it down, maybe check the vocab, then start practicing alone. Sure, this is going to feel like a lot of work (and a bit staged) but when you are in the situation that you can actually use your 'party piece of the week' you're going to feel so confident about it being right - and *boom* you've chalked up another little language victory! High five to you!

...but don't stop there. Create another phrase that could be frequently used and get polishing ready for your next victory! Follow this little plan and the more you do it the sooner you will be that confident Spanish speaker... guaranteed!

Linking your sentences together

In the early days of learning Spanish we focus a lot on the basics of the language - remembering which words are masculine and feminine, our regular verbs, that describing words follow the item etc..

Soon it becomes time to start putting the pieces of the jigsaw together and one of my frequently asked questions is "how can I learn and remember all those little linking words?" - to which I usually recommend compiling a list of these all-important words that will complete our sentences.

In fact, here's one I prepared earlier!

SPANISH	ENGLISH
a	to/at
en	in/on
de	of/from
o	or
y	and
un / una	a (m/f)
el / la	the (m/f)
los / las	the (pl. m/f)
unos / unas	some (m/f)
con / sin	with-without
si	If/yes

Getting these onto flashcards is always my go-to suggestion for swift learning (English on one side, Spanish on the other) but equally a list in the back of your vocab book works well.

Be sure to visit them often until they feel really familiar and sentence forming will become so much easier. Keep adding to your list as your repertoire expands.

Capital letters...

The use of **capital letters** is a common question raised in class.

The use of capitals (**mayúsculas**) is less frequent in Spanish than it is in English, so there are quite a few instances where you might instinctively expect to use one where it isn't actually needed.

Fortunately, I have some handy rules to help work out when and when not to use them...

DO use a capital letter...
- To start a sentence
- For names and surnames
- Countries, towns, villages

DON'T use a capital letter...
- Days of the week
- Months of the year
- Job titles - such as manager, doctor, president
- Long book/film titles: *The Lord of the Rings* becomes **El señor de los anillos** (first word only)
- Nationality and geographical reference. **Idioma español** – *the Spanish language*.
- The word **yo** prior to a verb. *I speak English* becomes **yo hablo inglés** (unless at start of sentence).

This, that, these and those...

Rule alert!

This is a topic that often causes a little confusion, so in class we use the following matrix...

THIS		**THAT**
esta	feminine	esa
este	masculine	ese
THESE		**THOSE**
estas	feminine	esas
estos	masculine	esos

As with so many things in Spanish, we first have to decide if our subject is masculine or feminine. Let's look at an example...

Let's imagine you wanted to say "this house" (not "a house", but specifically "this one"). The word for house is **casa** (and its feminine), therefore **esta casa.** Following the table above, "that house" would be **esa casa**.

Another example: "these books". We know that "book" is **libro** (and masculine), therefore **estos libros**. "Those books" would be **esos libros**.

TOP TIP:

If you look a little more closely at these pairings, you might spot a pattern. It can help to use the little saying *"keep 'T' close"*.

Going back to our first example

- **esta casa** - this house (here)
- **esa casa** - that house (over there)

The house which is closer to me (this house) has a 'T' in **esta**. The house which is further away (that house) has no 'T' in **esa**.

Hence the saying *"keep 'T' close."* When I'm referring to an object close to me, I add a 'T' to the word... and when it's further away, it's the same word without the 'T'. Cool, right?

The tale of a little dog...

Top Tip!

Here's a new word for you: **Diminutives**. I know, I hate "grammar chat", so to put that another way "making things smaller."

Now, this is really clever...

Let's say for example you wanted to talk about your "little dog". We take the word for dog (**perro**) and add **ito** (meaning "a small version of") to create the new word **perrito** (a little dog or puppy).

Essentially, adding **ito** (or **ita** if the item is feminine) to the end of the word creates a smaller version of that thing. Here are some more examples...

- (book) libro + ito = **librito** (small book)
- (cat) gato + ito = **gatito** (small cat or kitten)
- (bag) bolsa + ita = **bolsita** (small bag)
- (beach) playa + ita = **playita** (small beach)
- (house) casa + ita = **casita** (small house)

You can have lots of fun with this. Think of a word, check if its masculine or feminine and add your **ito / ita**! For example, jokingly in a restaurant... *"darme la cuentita"* (give me the bill, but only a little one!)

Go on, give it a try!

Sometimes find yourself lost for words in a conversation? Don't panic!

Top Tip!

There will inevitably be times when you start to use your new language and your mind just goes blank. You can't remember the right word, the sentence formation, maybe even the right tense to use. Argh!

The secret is **not to panic** (because the brain then reacts by zoning you out!) Worse still, don't give in and switch to English! A little trick I love to use that gives you a few little moments of thinking time is the word **pues** (pronounced "pwez"). It literally means "well..." or "ummmm..."

Using **pues** is *very* Spanish and buys you a seconds for the right words to pop into your mind! You can actually use it quite often...

- **¿qué quieres beber?** (what would you like to drink?) - "pues....."
- **¿dónde quieres comer?** (where do you want to eat?) - "pues....."
- **¿hay un supermercado por aqui?** (is there a supermarket around here?) - "pues....."

Give it a try, you'll sound like a native Spanish speaker!

Grab yourself a whiteboard!

Top Tip!

More and more of my students are using **whiteboards** at home to consolidate their learning.

Maybe park it by the kettle so that you can "swot" while you are waiting for it to boil (like student Tricia!), or alongside the running machine in the garage whilst you're burning those calories (like student Sarah!)

You'd be amazed how much repeatedly looking at the "learning of the moment" on your whiteboard during down time actually speeds up the learning process. Where would you place your whiteboard if you had one?

Everyone learns differently, so you should start where best suits you.

I regularly meet with students who are at varying stages of their Spanish learning journey. There are so many learning options out there, and in some cases they may have already tried quite a few of them.

- Evening classes
- Using an app
- Books
- Online tutorials
- CDs
- Language schools

Somehow they've not yet found the right way to learn. Something just hasn't yet "clicked" and we start down the route of 'how do I choose?"

When the time is right

I believe that timing is a major factor. Once you have decided that the time is right and you have a mindset to make it happen, all the other stuff that may have distracted you previously (work, family commitments, time, cost etc) becomes less important. Maybe something happens to bring on that change like moving to live Spain, the desire to travel in Spanish-speaking countries or simply "I need to master this!"

What next?

Sometimes people tell me they have come across my program, maybe via social media, and say they really like what they have seen but feel starting right at the beginning would just be too basic. They may have already collected lots of random "words" and don't really know how to string them together. Possibly they have been using verbs in their full form as they've not understood how to do otherwise.

It is for situations exactly like this that I created my "where are you at" questionnaire. I've mentioned it before in this book. It's a short "test" (in the least scary sense) that prospective students can complete – designed to show how much they already know, and where their gaps are. Everyone teaches and learns in different ways, but the paper allows me to decide where they might fit into my structured program. I can then recommend that they join an active class at that level. There's nothing more dispiriting that sitting through a class thinking "I already know all this..."

This has worked brilliantly for students who have completed the assessment to date and it is so rewarding to see them start to progress and really *enjoy* the learning process once again.

Why not take the test yourself?
You can download my "where are you at" questionnaire for FREE by scanning the barcode with your phone's camera. Don't be scared! It doesn't matter if you get things wrong or don't know the answer. The idea is to assess how much you know (or don't!) so that your lessons can be tailored to suit you.

To know... (part one)

In English, that sounds quite straightforward and innocent, but in Spanish it takes another one of "Janet's Rules" to tackle this one, mainly due to the fact that there are *two* verbs which both mean "to know".

Let's look at the first one, **conocer** and its list...

CONOCER

yo conozco
tú conoces
él / ella conoce
nosotros conocemos
vosotros conocéis
ellos / ellas conocen

(Did you notice that line one is irregular?)

To separate our two verbs with the same meaning – think of this one as **being acquainted with a person, place or thing**. Take a look at these examples:

- **yo conozco muy bien a Pedro**   *I know Pedro very well* (note that when we know a person, an "a" goes in front of their name)

- **nosotros conocemos Londres**   *We know London.* (meaning we've been there, we are familiar with it)

- **¿conoces las obras de Shakespeare?**   *do you/are you acquainted with the works of Shakespeare?*

Maybe you're thinking "acquainted with" is not the English term you would have used in these sentences, but as we move in the next "to know" verb, you'll see how this rule does actually help.

Keep an eye out for part two of this lesson later in the book. Spoiler alert, the second verb is **saber**.

How much & how many?

Here is another little area that always comes back to the subject of masculine & feminine. Don't I keep saying how important this topic is in the Spanish language?!

The word for how much/how many is **cuánto/a(s)**. It looks complicated, but it's not really. Let me show you...

If I wanted to ask "how many children do you have?" the subject that I'm enquiring about is *the children* (therefore **hijos**). That word is masculine & plural, so the questioning word picks that up and our question becomes...

¿cuántos hijos tienes?

Next I will ask "how much wine do you want?" Now because **vino** is masculine and singular, I would say...

¿cuánto vino quieres?

Here are some more examples:

¿cuántas personas hablan inglés aqui?
how many people here speak English?

¿cuánta comida está en la nevera?
how much food is in the fridge?

¿cuántos libros tienes que comprar?
how many books do you have to buy?

My Top Tips for speaking Spanish just like a native...

One of the best compliments a language learner can receive is being confused for a native speaker. It's one of those things that really gives you a buzz. So as a Spanish student how can you take your communicating abilities to the next level and fool others into thinking you're actually from Spain? Read on and I'll share some of my little secrets with you!

1. Use expressions
The Spanish have loads of expressions that they slip into their conversations. It's rare to hear a conversation that doesn't start with one of these. Trying working them into your conversations..

NO SÉ PERO... I don't know but ...
MIRA... Look...
A VER... Let's see...
LO QUE PASA ES QUE... What's going to happen is...
SABES (LO QUE TE QUIERO DECIR)... You know (what I mean)...

2. Use your hands
Ok this is visual rather than vocal, but have you ever observed a Spanish person when they are talking? Their hands are generally working as hard as their tongues!! Observe the different gestures they use and see how many you can adopt. Likewise movement of the head and eyes play a large part of their general body language when talking. This will also have you 'looking like' a Spaniard, as well as sounding like one!!

3. Cut the formality
Despite what our parents told us, the Spanish do not feel the need to use "please" and "thank you" as often as we do. It's not rude to drop it from our conversation, it's their culture that says it's just not necessary – just as it is ours that says it is. They sometimes feel that "over using" it can dilute how genuine the feeling is. So save it for special occasions!

If a Spaniard says thank you to you, you should follow it up with a **de nada** (you're welcome), as is their culture .

My Top Tips for speaking Spanish just like a native... continued

4. Use some fillers

No, not that kind. Every country and every language has its own *conversational* fillers. In English, we say things like "um..." or "you know..." In Spanish they have their own collection too. Here are some common ones:

Eh... This is the equivalent of "um..."
Pues... also means "um..."
Bueno... Well...
O sea... I mean...
A ver... Let's see...

5. Get excited

The Spanish are very passionate, emotional people. It always sounds like they're mad or angry, when in reality they're not. They could be excited, upset, or just merely saying "good morning" to their neighbour.

So don't be afraid to be more emphatic when you speak. Get excited, let your emotions come out! It's okay, everyone else is doing it too!!

6. Explain like a native

Here's a little trick that'll make you sound like a local (or at least someone who really understands Spanish culture) without a lot of effort. Spaniards often start phrases with **"es que..."** when they want to give an explanation. Roughly translated it means "it's because". Here are some examples of how it's used:

Perdón por no llamarte. Es que he tenido mucho trabajo esta semana...
Sorry for not calling you, I had a lot of work this week...

¿Quieres ir al cine este finde?
Would you like to go to the movie during the weekend?
No, perdón. Es que estoy ayudando a mi amigo con la mudanza.
No, sorry. I'm helping my friend with a move.

To be or not to be...

...that is the question, indeed. If you are learning Spanish via classes, apps, YouTube or whatever route, I am sure that you have encountered the verbs **SER** and **ESTAR**, both essentially meaning "to be". If you are like the majority of students, you have probably found them a bit challenging.

Most students are taught that **SER** is for the *permanent* things in life and **ESTAR** is for the *temporary* things in life. The black and the white. However when I was learning, all too often things fell into the grey areas, leaving the dilemma of "well, should I use SER or ESTAR?"

So I set about devising some guidelines for myself which would help to eliminate those grey areas and make everything easier to decide.

Let's start with **SER** for now. I always try to avoid too many grammatical words or phrases. *Keep it simple* is my motto! Not in any kind of patronising way, simply that students seem to prefer it that way. So when "listing", the verb SER it looks like this...

Yo **soy**		I am
Tú **eres**		you are
Él/ella **es**		he/she/it is
Nosotros **somos**		we are
Vosotros **sóis**		you (plural) are
Ellos/ellas **son**		they are

That's the "how" to use it. Equally important to learn and perfect is the "when" to use it! Here's what I came up with:

Description - when you are describing something or somebody

Origin - when you are talking about where someone is from

Character - someone's character, on a day to day basis what are they like

Time/date - when talking about what time/day/month/date it is etc

Occupation* - what somebody 'does'. Their job, retired, student, housewife etc

Relatives* - also including friends & neighbours

We actually refer to this affectionately in class as "the doctor list!" As we progress, you'll see that there is also a version of the doctor list for the ESTAR verb too.

I believe that learning this list is as important as the list of the verb itself because once perfected, you'll easily be able to decide the right verb to use without long pauses and uncertainty in the flow of your conversation.

*These were two areas that really confused me when I was studying. How can an occupation be permanent? I've changed my job many times,. friends come and go, how can they be permanent? We'll explore that "why" later in the book...

"Do" & "Don't" don't exist!

Do you remember me saying previously that the word "do" doesn't exist in Spanish? Instead we use the upside-down question mark or the intonation in our voice to denote a question.

hablas inglés
you speak English

¿hablas inglés?
do you speak English?

See how the Spanish for those two is exactly the same?

In a similar way, "don't" doesn't exist either. Instead the word **no** is placed in front of our verb. Why? Well, this turns the verb's action from a positive to a negative. For example…

Yo hablo Inglés
I speak English

Yo no hablo inglés
I don't speak English

Él paga la cuenta
he pays the bill

Él no paga la cuenta
he doesn't pay the bill

Nosotros comemos juntos
we eat together

Nosotros no comemos juntos
we don't eat together.

How a little French knife can help your grammar…

I know what you're thinking. "She's got another story here, hasn't she?" Yes. Yes I do…

When learning another language I find that students often get confused (and frustrated) by the "running order" of words when forming their own sentences - with describing words (adjectives) coming *after* rather than *before* the 'thing' (noun). It's "a green apple" but "una manzana verde", for example. There seems to be a lot of rules to learn. But many of us do not even give a second thought to our own native English and how many rules that has, especially around syntax (or "the order of words in a sentence").

For example, did you know that adjectives in English absolutely must be in this order: opinion – size – age – shape – colour – origin – material – purpose - Noun. Don't believe me? For example you can have a **"lovely little old rectangular green French silver whittling knife"**, but if you mess with the order of any one of those adjectives the whole sentence suddenly sounds *strange*. It's an odd thing that every English speaker uses that rule, quite naturally, but almost none of us could write it out!

My point is that, at some point, you learned that rule and it now feels quite natural and almost instinctive to you and you could immediately tell if someone put those adjectives in the wrong order. We will all have gotten it wrong, repeatedly, while we were learning to speak – we just don't remember.

The same will be true of learning a new language. The natural flow will come with practice… and we know that practice makes perfect!!

To be or not to be... (part 2)

Let's continue our journey of **SER** and **ESTAR**...

You'll remember that earlier we saw how using the letters of DOCTOR gave us pointers that we should be using the verb SER. How is that coming along for you? A little bit easier than the permanent / temporary rule you may have been using up until now?

As I mentioned, there is an anagram that serves the verb **ESTAR** in the same way, but before we get into that let's take a look at the listing for the verb...

Yo **estoy**	I am
Tú **estás**	you are
Él/ella **está**	he/she is
Nosotros **estamos**	we are
Vosotros **estáis**	you (plural) are
Ellos/ellas **están**	they are

That's the "how" to use it. Equally important to learn and perfect is the "when" to use it...

Position - where something or somebody is located

Location* - where a building or town/city etc is

Action - when the following verb ends in "ing" (e.g. I am studying - *estoy estudiando*)

Condition - the current status of something: hot water, cold soup, a dirty car etc...

Emotion - how someone is feeling: happy, sad, angry etc

So here we have an ESTAR version of SER's "Doctor list". Perhaps unsurprisingly, we refer to this in class as "the PLACE list." Again, I think it is equally as important as learning the listing for the verb itself.

Gaining control of when we use SER or ESTAR via these little "aide mémoires" will make your Spanish sound polished. It demonstrates to the listener that you have taken the time needed to understand the usage so you'll gain many more "respect" points!

Now, that said, I don't want to sugar coat the fact that if you can recite the list of DOCTOR & PLACE, you'll always be fine when using these two verbs. It's one of my classic **practice makes perfect** scenarios. There will be wobbles!

*Here we have a common dilemma: Take the sentence **"this coffee is hot"**. Is this a DESCRIPTION (therefore we'd use SER) or a CONDITION (therefore it's ESTAR)? Which do you think is correct? Read on for the solution...

Giving and asking for directions...

This is useful if you're trying to find a location, give directions in a taxi or arrange a delivery. Let's look at some basics first...

izquierda (left) This one looks a challenge to pronounce but let's break it down... *iz-key-air-dah*

derecha (right) *day-retch-ah*

sigues todo recto (carry straight on) *see-gez*

giras a la derecha/izquierda turn right/left

en la rotunda at the roundabout

en el cruce at the junction

primera/segunda first/second

en el semáforo at the traffic lights

Can you follow along with this conversation where I am giving directions to my taxi driver? Do we reach home?

- En el semáforo giras a la izquierda...
- Sigues todo recto hasta la rotunda...
- Giras a la derecha
- Sigues hasta el cruce y giras a la derecha...
- Mi casa está la segunda en la izquierda.

Talking about possessions

This might include physical items or family members, friends etc. Firstly, let's take a look at the 'list'...

- **mi** my
- **tu** your
- **su** his/hers
- **nuestro/a** his/her (depending if the 'possession' is m/f)
- **vuestro/a** your (pl) (depending if the 'possession' is m/f)
- **su** their

Now we have those, let's put them into practice...

- **mi coche** my car
- **tu hermana** your sister
- **nuestro perro** our dog (see how the nuestro has picked up the masculinity of the dog)

I remember one day in class a student asked me "how will I know when I hear "su" if the person is talking about *his* or *hers* or *their* item?" That's a good question! Did you spot that they are all the same?

The answer is quite straightforward though - in English or Spanish actually it's the same rule. In an actual conversation, you would have "set the scene" in advance of this sentence. For example:

Mi amigo es de Madrid, él tiene 40 años, él es medico y su esposa es enfermera
My friend is from Madrid, he is 40, he is a doctor and his wife is a nurse.

We've set the scene by giving details of my friend and then referred to HIS, and it can only be him.

Back to our possessions for the final point. Should those possessions become plural the 'list' is made plural too. Lets see that in action:

- **mis padres** my parents
- **tus niños** your children
- **sus libros** his/her books
- **nuestro/as amigos/as** our friends
- **vuestro/as hermanos/as** your (pl) brothers and sisters
- **sus clases** their classes

Dealing with double negatives...

This is something that takes a bit of getting used to in Spanish. In English, two negatives would make a positive – for example "I don't not like him", actually means "I do like him". It works slightly differently in Spanish.

Let's look at an example of what I mean...

Yo no nado nunca
I never swim

The literal translation is *I don't swim never* which to our English minds would imply that if I don't swim never, I must swim sometimes, right?!

It's a classic case of over-thinking! Something we simply have to avoid doing and accept that some things are just done differently in Spanish.

Certainly this is the case when we are using **nunca** (never) as in the example above. Here are a few more...

yo no bebo nunca el vino tinto
I never drink red wine

nosotros no comemos nunca el carne
we never eat meat

Ella no recuerda nunca mi nombre
she never remembers my name

Looking at our daily routine...

Talking about our daily routine is another subject which is good for those **intercambio** conversation practice sessions. It brings into use a group of verbs called **reflexive verbs**.

Now, let's quickly get "the technical bit" out the way so we can focus more on how they work.

Reflexive verbs are used when the subject (the person "doing" the action) and the object (the receiver of the action) are the same. For example "**I** wash **my** hair", "**he** brushes **his** teeth". Basically, reflexive verbs are for things we do to ourselves.

Here are some more examples:

- **me despierto** I wake up
- **me levanto** I get up
- **me ducho** I have a shower (technically, I shower myself)
- **me seco** I dry myself
- **me desayuno** I give myself breakfast

All these examples are AR verbs, so if you were asking someone else about their routine, you would need line two of the verb. See how the "who's who" changes from **me** to **you**, and the verb ending changes as is normal with our AR verbs.

- **te despiertas** you wake up
- **te levantas** you get you
- **te duchas** you have a shower

So a conversation might typically be...

¿a qué hora normalmente te despiertas?
what time do you normally wake up?

Normalmente me despierto a las 7 y me levanto
normally I wake up at 7am and I get up

> **CHALLENGE:**
> Have a go at putting together your own morning routine. Is it any different at the weekend? Take a look overleaf for more examples of daily routine reflexive verbs...

Looking at our daily routine...

me llamo

I call myself

me despierto

I wake up

me levanto

I get up

me ducho

I shower

me seco

I dry myself

me desayuno

I have breakfast

me maquillo

I put on make-up

me peino

I comb my hair

me visto

I get dressed

Looking at our daily routine...

me siento cansado

I feel tired

me desvisto

I get undressed

me baño

I have a bath

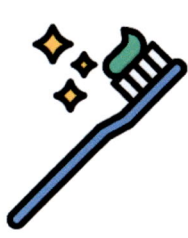

me cepillo los dientes

I brush my teeth

me pongo la pijama

I put on my pyjamas

me acuesto

I go to bed

me duermo .... horas

I sleep for ... hours

Por la mañana...

In the morning...

...a las [ocho]

...at [eight] o'clock

SER and ESTAR anomalies...

Earlier we looked at general teachings which split these two verbs into "permanent" and "temporary" categories... the black and the white. When I started to use the language I discovered a large grey area between the two with much that just didn't fit those classifications. That is why I went on to create the DOCTOR and PLACE lists, to alleviate any confusion.

Let me expand firstly with "occupations." During my life, I've had various occupations, so how could that be permanent? If you think back to when the language was evolving, if you had been born into a family of bakers there would be no "what are you going to be when you grow up?" You were a baker, you baked bread and your surname was probably Baker. That was that. You see how that might be classed as permanent, right?

The same is true with "relatives & neighbours." In times past, we were born into a family home. Parents, grandparents and children all in one house. You didn't move further than the village and everyone else was the same. Neighbours were permanent.

I also set you a challenge earlier about the cup of coffee. "It is hot." Is that **ser** or **estar**? This challenge often arises, am I *describing* it (therefore **ser**) or is it a *condition* (requiring **estar**). The solution is ..

If I was saying "this is coffee" I am *describing* what the beverage is - therefore SER: **este es café**

If I was saying "this coffee is hot" I am stating the *condition* of it - therefore ESTAR: **este café está caliente**

How did you do with that?!

Obligations...

When we need to talk about things we *have* to do, (for example "I have to drink more water...") there is a convenient and helpful little formula to use to help us get it right.

When using this rule, try to avoid translating your sentence back into English in your mind once you have created it. It won't really make much sense when translated literally – you'll just have to trust me on this one!

There are three simple steps to remember with this rule...

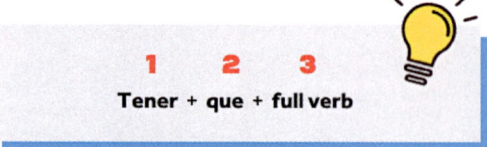

Tener + que + full verb

Simple enough, right? So let's see the rule in use. Remember we wanted to say "*I have to drink more water*"

- **Step one:** Select the YO line of the verb **tener**
- **Step two:** Add your "que"
- **Step three:** Add the full version of our verb, in this case it's **beber** (to drink)

All together now: **"tengo que beber más agua..."**

Now you've got the hang of it, let's look at another example: *"I have to go to the bank"*.

Using our three steps... **"tengo que ir al banco"**

So there you have it. A simple rule to remember how to say we "have to" do something. You might say it's a simple as 1...2...3...!

To know... (part two)

A few pages back we were looking at how there are two verbs which mean "to know". Let's look at the second one, **saber** and its list...

SABER

yo sé
tú sabes
él/ella sabe
nosotros sabemos
vosotros sabéis
ellos/ellas saben

Did you notice that, as with **conocer**, line one is irregular? Top tip: learning that YO line will come in really useful, we use it so much!

Si, yo lo sé *yes, I know* (or literally, yes I know it)
No lo sé conversely, *I don't know* (it)

So, back to the verb. **Saber** is used when talking about **facts**, in contrast to **conocer** which is used if we are **acquainted with** a person/place/thing. For example:

yo conozco muy bien a Pedro
I know Pedro very well (I am acquainted with him)

yo sé que Pedro vive en Barcelona
I know that Pedro lives in Barcelona (fact)

sabemos que él le gusta viajar
we know that he likes to travel (fact)

Notice the difference? By thinking **acquainted with** and **facts**, it allows you to think more quickly as to which verb is applicable.

Saber also has a second use, when we are talking about **knowing how to do something**. All that is needed is a simple two-part formula to achieve this: **Saber + full verb** (of the activity). For example:

Yo sé cocinar paella   I know how to cook paella
Yo sé tocar el piano   I know how to play the piano
Yo no sé reparar coches   I don't know how to repair cars

Try not to be tempted to do a literal translation (for example that first sentence literally means "I know to cook paella", which feels like it is missing the "how". Ignore that fact (and the need to ask why), it's just the way it is!

Ser & Estar

How are those two verbs **SER** and **ESTAR** coming along for you?

Didn't I say they were going to be one of the biggest challenges in the language?

Anything that can help them "stick" in the mind gets my vote. That's why I love to share the DOCTOR and PLACE lists - do you remember those from earlier?

Likewise, I find this happy little verse is catchy enough to stay in the head and help us even further...

"

How you feel and where you are,

That is when you use ESTAR!

I'm hungry...

There are several phrases in Spanish that use **tener** ("to have") where we would use "to be" in English. For example, instead of the English "being hungry", in Spanish we *"have hunger."*

"But why?" I hear you ask... On this occasion it's one of those "that's just the way it is" situations. It is simply a part of how the Spanish language is constructed (and actually also most of the other European languages that have Latin in their history – if anything, the way we do things in English is the exception!)

Therefore, **I'm hungry** becomes **tengo hambre** (pronounced ten-go AM-bray). Literally, "I have hunger."

Are you hungry? becomes **¿tienes hambre?** (pronounced ti-EN-ez AM-bray).

As I mentioned, there are several phrases which work in this way, where in Spanish we "have" something rather than "being" something. Take a look at a few of the more commonly used examples...

- **Tener sed** - to be thirsty
- **Tener calor** - to be hot
- **Tener frio** - to be cold
- **Tener suerte** - to be lucky
- **Tener razón** - to be right

Two fewer words to learn...

Did you know that the words **do** and **don't** do not exist in Spanish? That means you have two fewer words to worry about!

So what about asking someone a question? Or giving an answer? Read on...

As a famous comedian once said *"it's the way I tell 'em!"* and that's pretty much the story with asking questions in Spanish. You may have noticed that Spanish sounds very "musical" when being spoken by a native speaker. That's because so much of the content is expressed by the intonation, or the rise and fall, of the voice. It's by mastering that musical way of speaking that we sound less like we are reading from a textbook and more like a local. That is our ultimate goal, but for now lets get back to asking questions...

In Spanish, the statement "you speak English" is **tú hablas inglés**, but what if we wanted to ask the question "*do* you speak English?" Well, we have already seen earlier in this book that, if it was in written form, the question marks **¿?** are wrapped around a sentence and it becomes a question... **¿tú hablas inglés?**

In the spoken form the words are exactly the same, but said with a questioning tone in our voice, making the statement now sound like a question.

To create the reply "I don't speak English" without using the word **don't** (because that doesn't exist either!) we simply place a "**no**" in front of our verb... **yo no hablo inglés.**

So you see, it really is "the way you tell 'em..."

Is your motivation in hibernation?

I know it's tricky to get motivated sometimes. As I sit and write this, we are experiencing lockdown and a global pandemic. The restrictions, missing loved ones (which all seems never ending) and to top it all the weather too has been rubbish this week! Knuckling down to your studies probably feels like a step too far right now - it's no wonder you feel as flat as a pancake!

That's why I've written my **top tips** to tackle motivation hibernation. Different things work for me at different times, so take a look and see if any of these feel appealing or even vaguely doable. I've used them all at various times as I know they're guaranteed to get me dusting off my workbooks and getting into study mode.

- **Be kind to yourself:** if your number one tactic is beating yourself up because you're not doing what you are supposed to... maybe stop that?
- **Tackle your least favourite topic first:** no excuses, grab a coffee and dive in to a little revision on that subject. Once you've done it you'll feel so chuffed with yourself. You've started!
- **Tackle your favourite topic first:** reverse psychology - if you're not feeling brave enough to tackle the above, ease back in a little more gently with something that you really feel confident with and glance through those notes. This used to be a new/tricky subject and now it's on your favourites list. Whether you choose favourite on least favourite topic, the key is that you're taking that first step.
- **Do a brain dump:** make a list of the subjects you feel you still need to master. Is that a past tense or maybe a future tense? Is SER and ESTAR still challenging you? Do you need more conversation practice? Get it all down on paper and you'll then have a plan of attack for this term/year. Now action: is there a workshop on my website that meets those needs?
- **Pick a sticky note:** I love my Post-Its! Take five notes and write a short everyday Spanish phrase on each. Each day pick one post-it and that's your phrase (or piece of vocabulary) for the day. This is great for getting you back in the swing and building your confidence too.
- **Give yourself a structure:** decide what time of day is your best time for learning and plan in say, three sessions a week. Put it on the calendar and plan any other activities around those sessions. It only need be half an hour, but commit to it. Once you're into the routine, the sessions fly by and you will start to see real progress.
- **Think about WHY you are learning Spanish:** what was your motivation to start learning? As a hobby? Because you're living in Spain? For your children? Does this still apply? Let's keep going!

As I said at the beginning, cherry pick those that you think will work for you. The main thing is to **do something**. Just taking one step today and another tomorrow, and you'll be on your way. If not, you can always contact me for ideas to help you refocus with your learning.

Looking into the future...

Top Tip!

I am often asked by students *"how can I make my Spanish sound more natural?"* In the early days of learning the language, we spend a fair slice of time talking in the present tense in order to learn the basic essentials of how the language "works". Things like getting your pronunciation right, putting describing words after the subject... and then there's all the verb related stuff...!

All the things we have been covering so far in the book will help you to build a strong foundation in the language. However it is when we start weaving in some **future** and **past tenses** that the language really starts to come alive. What's equally important is that we start to understand more and more of what we are hearing. A good place to start is with the future tense. Think about how often we talk about things that haven't happened yet, or will be happening in the future...

- Where are you going at the weekend?
- Is he going to pay the bill?
- I am going to clean the car later
- They are going to work in the garden

Note that each of these sentences, in English, contains the word **going**. These activities are not yet happening, but are **going to happen**. I want you to think of the word **going** as a trigger. My little "1..2..3...Going" formula is really helpful for talking about some future activity.

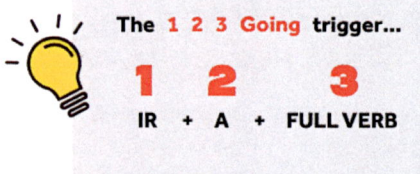

The **1 2 3 Going** trigger...

1 + **2** + **3**
IR + A + FULL VERB

1. take the line of the verb IR for who is doing this activity
2. is always "A"
3. is the full verb for the activity

Now we've got that little rule in our heads, let's go back to those previous sentences and add their Spanish translations...

- Where are you going at the weekend?   ¿dónde **vas a ir** el fin de semana?
- Is he going to pay the bill ?   ¿él **va a pagar** la cuenta?
- I am going to clean the car later   **voy a limpiar** el coche luego
- They are going to work in the garden   ellos **van a trabajar** en el jardin

This little rule works in exactly the same way if you are asking questions or making statements. As simple as one, two, three! Getting started on it is the key. Like everything, it takes a bit of thinking about at the start. Something I recommend a lot is to practice during your self-chat. Start your day with one of the following. Give it a try!

- I am going to eat cereals for breakfast   **voy a comer** los cereales para el desayuno
- What am I going to do today?   ¿qué **voy a hacer** hoy?
- I am going to wear my white t-shirt   **voy a llevar** mi camiseta blanca
- Later I am going to go to the bank   luego **voy a ir** al banco

What I want...

The verb "to want" in Spanish is **querer**. How are you doing with the pronunciation on that one? It often causes issues! Think of it as *care-air*, and you'll have it just about right. Let's have a look at its list...

QUERER

- **yo** quiero
- **tú** quieres
- **él/ella** quiere
- **nosotros** queremos
- **vosotros** queréis
- **ellos / ellas** quieren

What can we tell from this list? Well, the verb is irregular (the stem has picked up an 'i') and it is a "boot verb" (the stem on nosotros/vosotros is the same as the full verb). Don't worry, we'll take a closer look a boot verbs later in the book...

This verb is really useful when we are shopping, in a restaurant and generally when we are talking about our wants (or don't wants). For example:

- **queremos una mesa para cuatro**   we want a table for four
- **él quiere ser un medico**   he wants to be a doctor
- **¿qué quieres?**   what do you want?
- **quiero dos bocadillos de atun**   I want two tuna rolls
- **ella quiere un coche nuevo para su cumpleaños**   she wants a new car for her birthday.

You may be thinking that some of those phrases sound a little 'direct' when we translate them to English. "Please" and "thank you" are very rarely used in Spain. Not because they are bad mannered, they simply don't think it necessary as we've mentioned before. I found this quite challenging to overcome in the early days, *por favor* kept slipping out! Old habits die hard !!

Until I discovered **queria** (care-RIA). It comes from **querer**, but is a softer version – more "I would like" than "I want".

- **yo queria una copa de vino blanco**   I would like a glass of white wine

That definitely sat better and felt more like me! It's a personal choice, the Spanish really don't worry. So take your pick and start telling them what you want. A *full sentence* when you're next in a restaurant rather than just 'vino blanco'(!)

Oops I've made a mistake!

As I've said, making mistakes is part of the learning journey. It's all part of how we learn and grow. Sometimes our pronunciation is not quite on point or we've used the wrong verb... you can read their body language; they have NO idea what you have just said!

Rule number one
Don't panic, this just scrambles the brain! Simply move quickly on to...

Rule number two
A verb that I love which can be used to lighten the mood and get you out of this situation is **equivocarse** (ecky-bow-CAR-say) "to make a mistake." Doesn't that just roll off the tongue!

¿me he equivocado?
have I made a mistake ?

Or, if you know where you went wrong, you could use...

¡ups, me he equivocado!
whoops! I've made a mistake!

Don't you love that **ups** means whoops?!

Some notable exceptions...

Let's go back to one of those rules we were looking at earlier. How are your pots 1, 2 and 3 coming along... are you getting to grips with the masculine and feminine challenge?

My little "rules" help us along in most situations, but there are occasions when I mutter the word *however*... (eyes normally turn to the ceiling at this point in class!) This is one of those moments.

I mentioned at the end of the feature on masculine and feminine that there are a few exceptions. They are very few in number, but they are out there - and this time there *is* a reason why! Let me show you...

Let's look at **leche** (milk). It should belong in Pot 3 because it doesn't end in A or O. It should therefore be **el leche**, but just try saying that - "el leche" - those two "L"s together really fight against each other. Your tongue has to dance some kind of salsa. No, it just doesn't run smoothly and is very "un-Spanish". So they make an exception to **la leche**. That's much neater to say!

Another example is **agua**. Following the rules, that should be in Pot 1, "**la agua**". Again, those two A's clash in the mouth, so again an exception is made to **el agua**. Super neat!

It's all about making the pronunciation **smooth**. If you see something written that shows an "el" where you are expecting a "la", try saying it out loud and test what I am saying. This rule is very similar to our own English language rule that changes "a" to "an" before a vowel (because "an egg" is much smoother than "a egg"). Same reason!

Don't lose sleep worrying about a mountain of exceptions. They will come up, but very infrequently.

...one final exception

While we are looking at Masculine vs. Feminine, let's look at one last exception...

This little rule focuses purely on Pot 3 - the one with all the words that don't end in A or O.

More specifically, we're looking at **all words that end in a Z**.

Lets look at an example "**lápiz**" (pencil) is **el lápiz** (pronounced LAA-PITH, the Z is like the English TH sound).

If a word ends in Z, we still add the "es" when we are making it plural (as per the normal Pot 3 rule) but this time the Z changes to a C.

So the plural of **lapiz** becomes **los lápices** (los LAA-PITHEZ)... the CE is again pronounced like the English TH.

Another example is **el náriz** (the nose). That becomes... yes, you've got it... **los nárices**.

You'll be pleased to hear that there aren't a huge number of words which end in Z – but forewarned is forearmed! Just an extra little trick to have up your sleeve...!

It's a back to front world...

Things will rarely run in the same order in Spanish as they do in English – and that is especially true when looking at constructing a sentence.

We learn early on that **describing words follow the thing they are describing**. For example...

- **el coche blanco** - the white car
- **la casa blanca** – the white house

Well that all seems pretty simple, right? Not so fast! There are some instances where some Spanish describing words come before the thing they are describing.

This is because some common describing words have a different meaning depending on whether they come before or after the item. Depending on where they land in the sentence, our describing words can change.

Let's look at some examples ..

- **Un nuevo sombrero -** a new (different) hat
- **Un sombrero nuevo -** a (brand) new hat

- **Un gran hombre -** a great man
- **Un hombre grande -** a large, big man

- **La pobre niña -** the poor (unlucky) girl
- **La niña pobre -** the poor (not rich) girl

- **Varias personas** - several people
- **Personas varias** - various (diverse) people

Interesting, eh?

Take note of this when you are reading. How is the describing word changed by being placed in front of the item?

Vocab clusters

Over the years, as part of my own education (I was a newbie once too!) I have found that a good tip is to study vocabulary systematically on those topics of special interest to you. For example you might decide to focus in on a subject such as...

- Going to the doctor or vet
- Visiting a Spanish hairdresser
- Buying supplies at the ferreteria
- Getting your vehicle serviced
- Your weekly grocery shop

First up, research that subject inside and out (use a dictionary, an online translator, a Spanish friend). For example, let's look at that first idea, "the doctors", you could learn parts of the body, describing painful symptoms etc.

Next, when you have made a good list of vocabularly, decant it onto individual flashcards - English on one side, Spanish on the reverse .

Finally, practice the life out of the subject until you feel polished!

If you've chosen a topic that's regularly on your 'radar', you are sure to use the vocabulary and being able to converse when you're next in that scenario will do wonders for your confidence - so choose your subject matter well!

How your home town can help with your Spanish conversations....

Talking about where we are from is always a good conversation topic if you're practicing with a Spanish friend or in an intercambio group. The Spanish love to hear about places in the UK. If they have travelled to the UK, it is generally to either London or Manchester it seems, so anywhere else is always of interest. Personally, I'm a born and bred Bristol girl – which is not high on the Spanish list of tourist destinations – so that was always a goldmine of handy conversation starters when I was starting out with making new Spanish friends.

"Where we are from" is a topic you can work on, plan out and add to as your repertoire and confidence grows. A word that you can use in a project like this is **hay**, meaning "there is/there are". (TOP TIP: pronunciation is generally the challenge with this one I find. It is pronounced like EYE, the H is silent, so avoid going for hay/hey sound. Simply think eye. It has many uses as well as talking about places, such as...

- **¿hay una farmacia por aqui?**   is there a pharmacy around here?
- **No, no hay**   no there isn't
- **Hay mucha gente en el restaurante**   there are many people in the restaurant

Getting back to describing our home towns, here are some more examples of **hay** in action...

- **Hay muchas casas, escuelas y cento comerciales**   there are many houses, schools and shopping centres.
- **Hay una catedral y un puente famoso**   there is cathedral and famous bridge.
- **Hay muchas empresas grandes en el centro de la ciudad**   there are many big businesses in the town centre
- **También hay un centro de ocio grande con restaurantes, cine y tiendas**   also, there is a large leisure complex with restaurants, cinema and shops

You could make this an ongoing project for a while, weaving in some describing words to make the content even richer, for example...

- **Hay muchas casas bonitas, escuelas grandes y un centro comercial fabuloso**   there are many beautiful houses, large schools and a fabulous shopping centre.

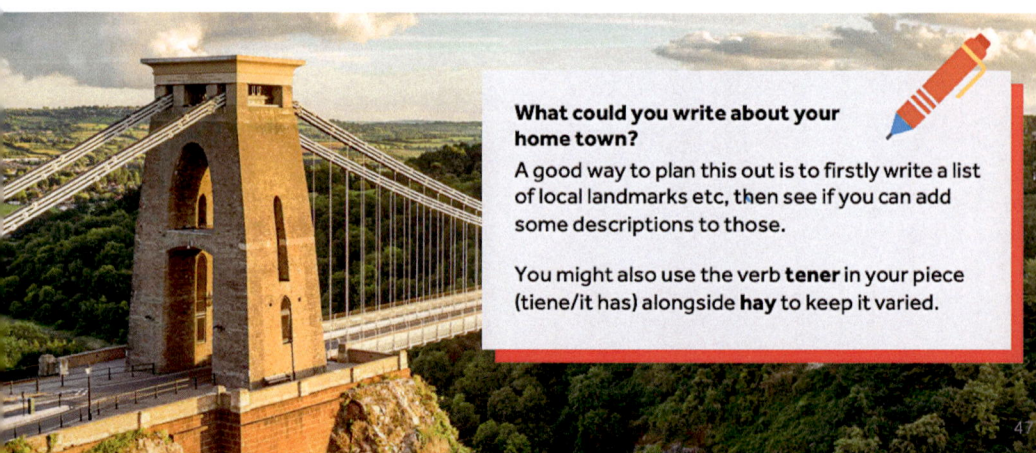

What could you write about your home town?

A good way to plan this out is to firstly write a list of local landmarks etc, then see if you can add some descriptions to those.

You might also use the verb **tener** in your piece (tiene/it has) alongside **hay** to keep it varied.

Learn your Spanish verbs in a FLASH!

Top Tip!

Love them or hate them, we soon discover that verbs are the backbone of the language.

We all study and learn in different ways and finding the way that works for you takes a bit of trial and error. Learning Spanish is a bit like getting your pilot's licence... you have to put in the flying hours to qualify.

"But I don't have time to sit and study verbs!" I hear you cry. Yes, I agree. It's not got a huge appeal factor. So the challenge comes in finding a method that can fit in to our hectic lifestyles that **makes learning fun** – if it's fun, we'll stick at it.

I believe the secret is **flashcards**. Small cards with the Spanish verb on one side and the English on the other.

Picture the scene. It's coffee time (or maybe my early evening glass of wine...) and my flashcards are at my side. English words facing up. My challenge is to turn over 10 cards (or 20 or 30, you choose your goal) and correctly guess the Spanish on the reverse. I work my way through, building my pile of "right" and "wrong". When I hit my goal, YAY!!! I get a chocolate biscuit (or another glass of red!) as my reward. It has become fun!

...and that's your "flying hours" clocked for today! You may choose to revisit your "wrong" pile later in the day, to refresh your memory, but this is an *anywhere activity* - walking the dog, in the queue in the bank, when you're on the sun-lounger. It has to be worth a try, right?

Age is just a number...

Over the years I have taught students of every age, from eight to eighty. One thing I can say for sure is that **age makes no difference at all to learning**. Ok, youngsters have youth on their side and can remember/recall a little faster, but if the mindset is right then achievement is possible... however old you are.

The important part is deciding (for whatever reason) that the time is right for you to learn. You *want* to do it now, rather than when you *had* to do it at school. This makes a world of difference! Never play "the age card" - just sign up for one of my Taster Classes and see how it goes!

Whilst we are on this subject...

When we are talking about age in Spanish, we speak of 'having' a number of years, rather than 'being'. For example:

I am 21 years old
yo tengo 21 años (I have 21 years)

To ask how old someone is...
¿cuántos años tienes tú?
"How many years to you have?"

Finally, correct pronunciation of the word year **(años)** is a strange one. Notice the "tilde" over the N? This causes the letter to be pronounced in a slightly different way. A "softer" or "rounder" sound, as if there is an invisible Y following the N. Phonetically, "ANN-YOS". So...

¿cuántos años tienes tú?

Let he who is without sin...

Do you see what I did there?!

From time to time, I am asked about the correct use of the word **sin** – the Spanish word for "without." It is however often (wrongly) interchanged with the word **no** instead.

This one fits into a nice, easy to learn rule. So let's take a look and see how it can help to bring some clarity...

The word **no** is generally used with a verb, turning a positive statement into a negative one, as in the following examples ...

- **No hablo español**   I don't speak Spanish
- **No como carne**   I don't eat meat
- **No vivimos en España**   we don't live in Spain
- **No puedes beber el agua**   you can't drink the water

But when we want to say things like "no problem" or "no milk (in my coffee)" when the sentence is translated into Spanish, we should use the word **sin**.

Let's take a look at some examples...

- **Sin problema**   literally, it is without problems
- **Sin leche**   coffee without milk
- **Sin dinero**   I'm without money
- **Sin duda**   literally, it is without doubt
- **Agua sin gas**   water without bubbles

It is quite logical if you think it through, just a bit different to what we are used to.

As I said, the "**no + verb**" is a general rule, and mostly holds true. The only notable exception is when we are referring to the opposite of yes... as in **no, gracias.**

The two ways of spending...

Hey, big spender!

Did you know that In Spanish there are two verbs which mean "to spend." Like with many things, it depends on specifically what we mean when we say we are "spending" something.

Let's have a closer look...

Use the verb **gastar** when we want to talk about spending **money**. For example...

- **No me gusta GASTAR mucho dinero** (I don't like to spend much money)

Alternatively, we use the verb **pasar** when are we spending **time**. For example...

- **Me gustaría PASAR un año en España** (I would like to spend a year in Spain)

Little tip - this second one may be easier to remember if you think of *passing* time.

Exactly WHO are you talking about?

¿Quién? is the Spanish questioning word for "who?"

Firstly, it's a word that is often mispronounced because, as English speakers, we are expecting to start with a *kwee* sound (as in Queen) but no, the correct pronunciation is KEY-EN. We emphasise the E as it has a tilde (remember that rule from earlier?) So now we have mastered how to say it, let's see how to use it...

Questioning words (who, what, where, when etc) will almost always start the sentence, preceded by the upside-down question mark. **¿Quién...** is then always followed by a verb. Here comes the top tip...

Let's think of a question we want the answer to. For example, we want to know if he/she does this activity - so logically we are going to use line 3, the he/she line, of our verb. Some examples...

- **¿quién habla inglés?**   who speaks English?
- **¿quién bebe vino blanco?**   who drinks white wine?
- **¿quién compra revistas?**   who buys magazines?

Sometimes it may be that two or more people are involved in the answer. In this instance - as we are now referring to *them* rather than a single *he/she* - we would use line 6 of the verb and **quién** becomes **quiénes.** Let's look at those same examples when we're expecting more than one person to say yes...

- **¿quiénes hablan inglés?**   who speaks English?
- **¿quiénes beben vino blanco?**   who drinks white wine?
- **¿quiénes compran revistas?**   who buys magazines?

Notice how the English version is totally unchanged, regardless of how many people we are talking about. So yes, we do need to think a little more when we're asking this question in Spanish – but it does quickly become automatic!

Extra note:
We won't always know whether one or multiple people are involved in the answer, but that's fine... simply stick with the single version. The general rule of thumb is

- Use line 3 or 6 of the verb with **¿quién / quiénes?**
- Or if in doubt, just use **¿quién?** + verb line 3

Typing tildes

Ever wondered how you can use tildes on your phone or tablet?

Using tildes (letters with an accent above them, such as **é** or **ú**) really shows respect for the language in the writing form. If you use your device to send emails in Spanish or just texting friends, it's so important to use grammar marks. Without them, the context of the word can be totally changed.

For example: **¿cómo?** means how? or what? However **como**, the same word without grammar marks, means "I eat!"

Back to typing on your mobile device. When using the keyboard, press and hold the letter you need to add a tilde to. A pop-up menu will appear, slide your finger across to select the accent you need.

Voila! Your **e** becomes an **é**!

Pleased to meet you...

This little story was a lesson for me in how making a mistake with your Spanish is not always bad news!

Early on in my own learning journey I'd been invited to meet some new friends so did a little bit of swatting up on my Spanish in advance of the meeting. *Google Translate* really wasn't a thing back then, so I resorted to my well-thumbed Collins Dictionary.

I had wanted to use the phrase "I'm pleased/it's nice to meet you", which I found to be **encantado**.

I remembered what my professor had taught me - things ending in 'o' meant I was talking about myself. So that all seemed to fit. I was ready. So off I set to meet my new amigos.

First off I was introduced to the husband of my Spanish friend. We did the customary mwah, mwah air-kisses and I spouted my **"encantado"**. He looked a bit taken aback, smiled and then proceeded to give me the full story of using this greeting...

There is an **encantado** and an **encantada** - masculine and feminine versions. The ending relates to the person *saying* the word. So I would always be encantada and he would be encantado!

The little story has never left me, more than 15 years on! For you, I hope it leaves you with two learning points...

1) how to greet people correctly and
2) never be afraid of having a go, maybe with a few mistakes and be ready to accept correction as a positive on your learning journey rather than a criticism.

As I say, every day's a school day!

The verb game

I believe it's important to make learning fun at every stage. The more you enjoy it, the more you want to continue.

I also recognise that at times *some* topics are plain hard work. All the more reason to find a way to lighten the load.

This is probably most true with **verbs**. Whether you are getting to grips with regular or irregular verbs, fun activities that involve you (and no notes!) will show what's actually going in and what needs more practice.

Here's a little game to make that activity fun and productive. You'll need a dice (**dado** in Spanish) and a pile of flashcards (or just a list) showing the verbs you are currently learning.

Remember back to when we were talking about the verb list? How a verb consists of 6 lines? Well we are going to use that thought for this game. (Spoiler: verbs have 6 lines, dice have 6 sides!) Here goes...

- Take the first flashcard from your verb pile. Let's say it's **cantar** (to sing).
- **Tirar el dado** (roll the dice). Let's say you roll a 3, therefore what is line 3 of the verb cantar?
- Write a sentence with this information... **ella canta muy bien** (she sings very well).
- Now simply repeat. You've rolled a 6 for the verb **estar**. Sentence example: **ellos están viviendo en una casa grande** (they are living in a big house)

Set yourself a target. Ten minutes on this activity three of four times a week will really crack those verbs. Even more fun when played with a study buddy!

Talking about our likes and dislikes

As our confidence grows, it's great to find Spanish friends to practice with. Certainly in tourist resorts there are loads of people working in the hospitality industry needing to speak English (and other languages) so equally they are also looking for an opportunity to practice too.

Keep an eye out in your area for any groups that meet in this way. These are generally called **intercambio de idiomas** or simply **intercambio** meaning *language exchange*. If there aren't any, why not start your own. I run regular sessions online called "Speak Easy" which you can find on my website. At these groups, initially the chatter is generally about ourselves - names, where from, family, work etc. All great, but where do we go next?

Sharing your likes and dislikes is a great step two and the verb we use to do that is **gustar.** It looks harmless enough, but it has a slightly different set of rules to learn, so let's dig a little deeper...

Here is the full "list" of the verb:

me gusta	**nos** gusta
te gusta	**vos** gusta
él / ella le gusta	**ellos / ellas** les gusta

You'll have spotted it has a new "who's who" list for starters, and the verb itself is unchanged through the whole list.

Although we are saying **me gusta** for "I like", the more accurate translation would be "to me...it gives pleasure." The verb or item which follows gusta is the thing or activity we like, or "gives us pleasure." For example...

- **me gusta el chocolate**   I like chocolate
- **me gusta la playa**   I like the beach
- **me gusta estudiar español**   I like to study Spanish
- **me gusta leer**   I like to read

So whether we are talking about liking things or activities, the **gusta** remains the same. However, hold your horses, there is nearly always an exception! If the "thing" we like is plural, the **gusta** becomes **gustan** (I know what you're thinking, we don't need to think about this in English!)

- **me gustan los zapatos**   I like shoes
- **me gustan las tapas**   I like tapas

But what about if we "dislike" something? The good news is that the rules are exactly the same, we simply add a **no**...

- **No me gusta whiskey**   I don't like whiskey
- **No me gusta nadar**   I don't like to swim
- **No me gustan las novelas romanticas**   I don't like romantic novels

In advance of your first intercambio session, why not write a list of your likes and dislikes (with single and a plural examples and also some verb examples). Then, as intercambio is an exchange of conversation, use the same set of rules to create some questions, like ¿te gusta la musica? ¿te gusta mirar las peliculas?

Why you should be a little more Amy and a little less Shirley...

Story time

A question I am often asked is "how can I improve my Spanish?"

Maybe you have been learning steadily for a period of time, studying as often as you can, and you feel like you've maybe reached a bit of a plateau?

It's time to take your courage in both hands and get out there and start putting your learning into action. So often I hear students say "Oh, I'm not quite ready yet" or "when I'm a little better, I will", but that day of being "ready" is like that light at the end of the tunnel that forever seems to be miles in the distance.

At times like this I often share this quote from American comedian, Amy Poehler...

"There's power in looking silly and not caring that you do."

I think that sums this up perfectly. Who cares if your verb is in the wrong tense, or you have mispositioned your adjective in front of your noun! Don't worry about looking silly, because it's through making mistakes that we learn and grow. Amy uses the word "power" whereas I prefer to call it "growth", but the two go hand in hand. Growth and advancement in the language come when you make a mistake, allow yourself to be corrected and learn from it, ready for next time.

Think of it like this: if a Spanish local was trying to talk to you in English (and maybe made a small error in their sentence), would you be more focussed on being pleased they were trying to talk to you in your language or on judging them for their mistake? Exactly.

Have you ever seen the movie Shirley Valentine? Shirley often finds herself "talking to the wall" as she spends a lot of her day alone. Is your wall your study buddy? (It used to be mine!) Your wall may be a great listener, but it's never going to help you with your pronunciation or strike up a mini conversation with you in Spanish to help boost your confidence!

You see where I'm heading with this? **Advancement comes with interaction.** Many students have discovered that having a few conversations with someone else who is learning Spanish is a far less daunting place to start. Very quickly we see those nerves evaporate and confidence grow. Time and again I see students leaving my conversation workshops (I called them "Speak-Easys") with the determination to finally start speaking "with the locals."

Give it a try. You'll be glad you did.

A quick look at POR and PARA...

Rule alert!

I'll be honest here, understanding the difference between these two can feel tricky, but like with any element of a language, mastering the difference between **por** and **para** just takes a bit of practice.

First, let me dispel a myth: one of the reasons you may find it complex is because Spanish learners are often told that por and para both mean "for." While this isn't wrong, it's not entirely true either...

There are many other translations for por and para in English and it all depends on the context. In an attempt to unravel the differences I use this graphic to help me remember which one I need...

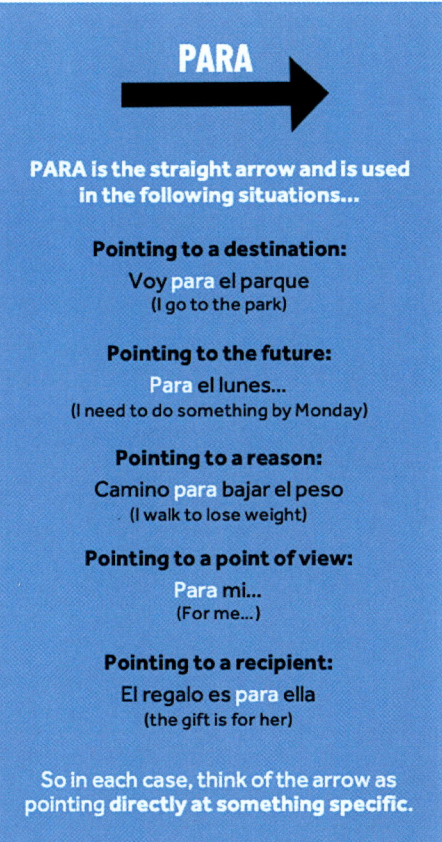

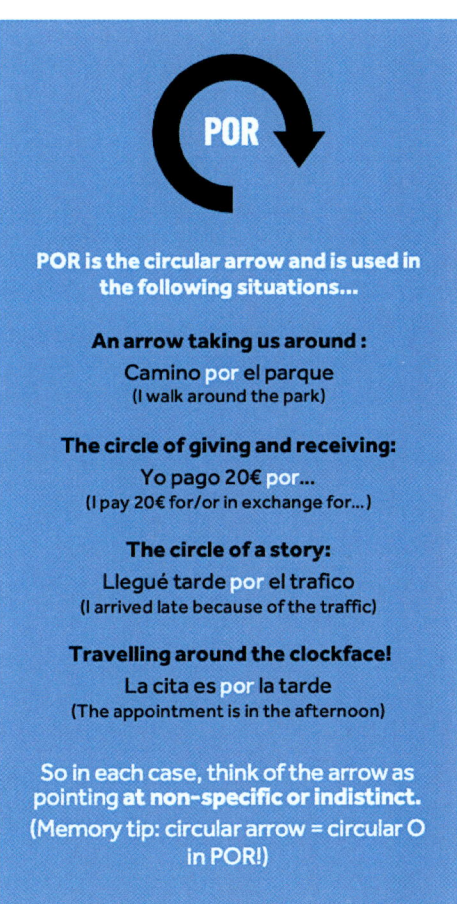

Yes I know, it's a bit of a headful! The arrows help to a degree but best way is to memorise them and of course **practice, practice, practice!**

Why you shouldn't be afraid to strike up a conversation...

I recently took a group of my students across to the neighbouring island of Gran Canaria to enjoy some retail therapy. Apart from the obvious enjoyment of browsing at a different shopping mall and indulging at lunch, I got to thinking about the numerous times I spoke Spanish during the day. The more I use it, the more I love the language and the spirited responses you get from the locals when they hear "foreigners" breaking into conversation with them.

Being out in a different environment, a short conversation can be struck up and BANG! Another little Spanish conversation to top up the confidence pot! Students often say that practicing isn't easy. Well yes, having a full debate on the state of the Spanish economy could be way off yet (should that ever be your thing!) but little bite-sized exchanges *will* pump up your confidence and get you moving towards bigger things. I've drawn together some conversation starters I use, for you to cherry pick a few (or more), to polish and perfect and make them your own! So here goes and in no particular order...

The "Change Fairy"

It seems that "small change" is in permanent short supply here on the island, so making the offer "would you like some change, I have lots of coins" will always get you a favourable response at your regular store. You could continue with "great! My purse is much lighter now!" I do this from time to time and before you know it you have a friend at the checkout... build on it each time you're there!

Different sizes

"Window shopping" becomes a whole new experience when you're wanting to practice your Spanish. When browsing you could ask the assistant if the style is available in a bigger/smaller size, or blue rather than pink etc. Any excuse for a quick chat!

The accent search

You might be thinking at this stage that all Spanish sounds alike! A little challenge is to listen for the word **gracias**. Here in the Canaries, you would hear GRA-SI-AS, whereas someone from Madrid for example would use the more lispy GRA-THEE-AS. Take the opportunity to ask where they are from, as their accent sounds different. Again, this often naturally turns into a conversation.

The "I think I might be lost" look...

I confess, I have been known to try this one more than once!! If I'm out, I pull up Google maps and appear to be searching for a street name or landmark. It always works! Someone will step up and offer help. Hello! A conversation opportunity has arrived! What places might they recommend I visit? Why? Any good restaurants? Whatever you like! The more often you try these, the easier and more confident you become.

Tips to improve your Spanish listening skills: Part 1

There are four parts to learning any new language: **reading**, **writing**, **speaking** and **listening**. The first and easiest to learn are usually the reading and writing. That's because you can *see* all the words you need to understand. You can take your time, study them and work them out in your own time. Improving your Spanish listening skills offers no such luxury. To make matters worse, Spanish is an incredibly fast-spoken language.

The good news? The more you exercise your brain with listening practice, the stronger it will get. There are more than a few ways you can quickly add some muscle to your brain with various Spanish listening activities. The first one is below, the rest are coming up later in the book.

Watch movies in Spanish with Spanish subtitles

Think of this like learning to ride a bike with the stabilisers on. It combines two areas of language learning – listening and reading. It allows you to follow along with what's being said without having to decipher only the spoken language.

Try this: One great exercise is to find a short scene with plenty of dialogue between two characters. Watch it with subtitles a few times until you can distinguish every word. Then watch it a few more times without the subtitles, listening carefully to the words and how they're spoken.

- Which points of the words are stressed?
- Where are the pauses?
- Which words or phrases are strung together to sound like a single word?
- Say the lines out loud as the characters says them. Do this enough times and you'll never forget how those certain words and phrases are pronounced.

Did you know many streaming services such as Netflix offer multi-language subtitles for many of their programmes? That means you can turn on Spanish subtitles to an English-language show.

A stem, a stem-change ...and a boot?!

What's that all about?! Don't worry I haven't gone mad!

This question comes up quite regularly with my students, so I thought it would be a good topic to share here. The question also often asked by students who may have been following an online teaching app or learning from books, as this subject (oddly) doesn't seem to be widely covered in the early stages of most programmes.

To explain: you'll likely already know that Spanish verbs end in either **AR**, **ER** or **IR** (for example, the verb hablar, meaning "to speak"). If we remove the AR, what is left (habl...) is called the stem.

Hablo
Hablas
Habla
Hablamos
Habláis
Hablan

When we write the full conjugated list of that verb, the stem remains unchanged.

Some verbs (called **irregular stem-changing verbs**) work differently. For example, the verb querer (meaning "to want"). Note how as we conjugate this verb, the stem changes...

An "i" is added to each line except for nosotros and vosotros (don't ask why, its just the way it rolls!!) I've written out the conjugated list of this verb with those two lines deliberately pushed out slightly to the right.

Quiero
Quieres
Quiere
    Queremos
    Queréis
Quieren

As a rule, on these two lines, the stem always returns to that of the original verb.

This style of listing an irregular stem-changing verb is also known as a **boot verb** because the outline (roughly) forms the shape of a boot! Pretty cool eh?

The changes to the stem on these verbs are many. It's a case of slowly but surely they go in! The one consistency? **On the nosotros and vosotros lines the stem will always return to that of the original verb.**

Tips to improve your Spanish listening skills: Part 2

As we saw earlier, it's a really good idea to add some muscle to your brain with various Spanish listening activities. Here are a few more of my favourite ways. Give them a try and see which works best for you...

Listen to Spanish songs
Music is a universal language and an excellent way to train your ears to listen to a foreign language.

This can be done easily via YouTube where you can also view and follow the lyrics. Other great places are Apple Music and Spotify – both of which will scroll the lyrics for you as the song plays, karaoke-style. A great way to follow along.

Watch the news in Spanish
This is a perfect opportunity to get a regular dose of daily Spanish and the great thing about the news is that it is (generally) very clearly spoken with minimum accent or slang.

Try this: For practice, watch a news clip and write down the important information: who, what, when, where and why. An excellent source for this is the BBC's Spanish-language news website, which has a large amount of video news that is clearly spoken and visually easy to follow.

Change your phone language to Spanish
Our phones are a huge part of our lives now and we use then all the time. It's amazing how much this small change will help you.

Try this: Head to the Settings area of your phone and you will find the option to switch to Spanish in the Languages section. (Be sure to remember the process so you can switch back to English when needed!)

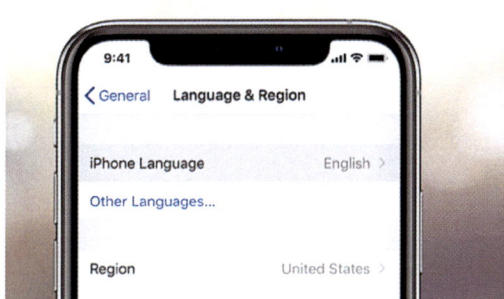

Why not use these few pages to make your notes. Your future self will thank you!

Why not use these few pages to make your notes. Your future self will thank you!

Why not use these few pages to make your notes. Your future self will thank you!

Why not use these few pages to make your notes. Your future self will thank you!

YOU'VE DONE BRILLIANTLY ...BUT DON'T STOP NOW!

Why not subscribe to my e-newsletter and receive hints, tips, learning activities and details of my upcoming online classes and workshops - completely FREE into your inbox each month.

You could even take your learning to the next level and sign up for one of my online Spanish language classes – at either beginner, intermediate or advanced level. Short taster courses are also available.

www.thespanishcoach.net/newsletter